Parent Power

Parent Power

Nourish 7 Essential Qualities Within Your Early Age Child

with

Kid M.E.A.L.S.

Messages **E**xercises **A**ctivites **L**essons **S**tories

LIFE SIZE lessons in kid size bites!

Written by
John R. Iannuzzi

Copyright © 2004 by John R. Iannuzzi

Book cover design and layout: Jacqui LeFranc

All rights reserved. No part of this book may be reproduced or transmitted in any form or by any means, electronic or mechanical, including photocopying, recording, or by any information storage and retrieval system, without permission in writing from the author.

This book was printed in the United States of America.

♦♦♦

Dedicated to the most important ingredients in my life

Kathie, John Ryan, Shane, and Maurina

♦♦♦

ACKNOWLEDGEMENTS

I'd like to acknowledge those who have taught me some of life's most valuable lessons... To my wife, Kathie, who taught me the meaning of unconditional love... to my seven-year-old son, John Ryan; four year-old-son, Shane, and seven month-old daughter, Maurina, who taught me the meaning of quality time... to my mom, Mother Teresa, who taught me that sacrificing really means gaining... to my dad, "Nipper," who taught me how to enjoy life... to my grandmother who taught me the meaning of "family"... to my twin brother, USAF pilot Lt. Colonel Philip A. Iannuzzi, Jr., who taught me the meaning of loyalty... to my sister, Jo-Ann, who taught me the value of friendship... to all the parents and educators I consulted with who taught me about qualities essential to a child's development... to Pam Durant and Melissa DiLeonardo who taught me about the craft of publishing and writing... to former colleague and veteran TV anchor, Larry Kane, who taught me the power of patience... to Dr. Richard R. Bocchini, Ph.D., who taught me what children really need... and to God, who taught me how to enhance the quality of time I've been given.

—John R. Iannuzzi

TABLE OF CONTENTS

Acknowledgements 7
Foreword 13

♦ First Course ♦

Introduction 17
Kid M.E.A.L.S. Overview 20

♦ Main Course ♦

1. SELF-ESTEEM 27
2. EMOTIONAL DEVELOPMENT 47
3. COGNITIVE SKILLS 67
4. HONESTY 83
5. SELF-RELIANCE 95
6. CREATIVITY 107
7. PURPOSE 125

♦ Last Course ♦

Conclusion 137
Index 139
References 149
About the Author 153

Greatest Love Of All

I believe the children are our future
Teach them well and let them lead the way
Show them all the beauty they possess inside
Give them a sense of pride to make it easier
Let the children's laughter remind us how we used to be . . .

—Whitney Houston

FOREWORD

The medium is the message.

—Marshall McLuhan

Accepting responsibility for the physical and emotional development of another human being is at best the ultimate challenge and if effectively carried out, provides the greatest of rewards. However, the changes taking place in our dual-income society is making it more difficult than ever for many of today's parents to accomplish this vital task. The effects of our over-worked and time-deprived culture pose a serious threat to the welfare of our children.

The dynamics that have taken place within the modern family structure are having an enormous effect on the way in which parents are raising their children. One consequence of this fact is the increased use of day-care and nanny services for young children. No one has yet studied in depth the outcome of this experience on the personal and emotional development of children. However, many parents are aware that the experiences their child has under someone else's care may not be the ones they would provide if they were a stay-at-home parent. These parents often feel at a loss as to how they might provide alternative experiences that are more closely related to their values—their ideas of personal behaviors and characteristics they would like to pass on to their children. In other words, one result of the loss of available parent-child time is that many parents are seeking ways and means of becoming more creative in how they use the time they do spend with their children. A significant aspect of being creative as we relate to our children is trying to develop the ability to recognize as well as to enhance special opportunities for learning life values.

Inside *Parent Power,* you will find a broad range of messages, exercises, activities, lessons, and stories, hence the term that John coined, M.E.A.L.S., which are designed to cultivate seven core qualities within early-age children. Once you read the activities you will find that they are unique, simple, and easy to use. For many parents, they offer a practical means of teaching their child life values. Additionally, these "meals" suggest ways, in which parents can engage their child with their own brand of messages, exercises, activities, lessons, and stories, that they deem important to their personal development. Of greatest significance is the fact that parents will enhance the quality of time they spend with them. Thus, the message delivered to the child [in this parenting resource] is twofold: I (we) as your parent(s) care enough about you to be involved with you on an emotional level, and these are the life values I (we) feel are important for you to learn.

—Dr. Richard R. Bocchini, Ph.D.
Child and Family Psychologist

Dr. Richard Bocchini has counseled children and families for over forty-years. He is also a founding director of the Child and Family Services Center that was established on behalf of the Pennsylvania Hospital's Community Health Care Program.

♦ First Course ♦

"Look, dear, the world."

INTRODUCTION

*Life affords no greater responsibility, no greater privilege,
than the raising of the next generation.*

—C. Everett Koop

Parents do everything they can to navigate their way through the demands of their daily routine. Yet, even if they approach each day with the coordination of a military tactician, inevitably some things get left behind. Making certain the personal development of their child does not become one of them is essential to the future of our next generation. But, that's a lot easier said than done.

As a father of three early-age children, whose spouse also works out of the home full-time, I speak from personal experience when I say parenting in a two-income household is an extremely challenging responsibility. Managing both work and family can be so time consuming, pressure filled, and exhausting, that many days just getting through it all is nothing short of amazing. However, whether you are raising a child in a single or double income household, such constraints on your ability to invest yourself in their development, needn't compromise the *quality* of time you spend with them.

For today's parents, achieving this goal has become a much more complicated affair than it had been in the past when a greater percentage of parents stayed at home. Parents are spending less time with their children primarily due to the changes that have taken place in the labor force over the past thirty years. As a result, the majority of parents are working and therefore spending significantly less time on the home front.

In 1974, the majority of children under the age of six spent an average of fifty-two hours per week with at least one parent, compared to thirty-nine hours per week by the year 2000. The number of households in which children are being raised by married parents who both work outside the home grew from 47 percent in the early seventies to over 70 percent by the turn of the century. More parents are working full time now than at any point in history. The bad news is that the changes in labor force are interfering with parents' ability to spend significant time interacting with their children. The good news is that parents are compensating by increasing the *quality* of time they spend with them to offset the lack of time.

Parents are spreading themselves so thin trying to make ends meet that they are forced to make choices, which ultimately will affect how their children are raised. Let's face it, whether you're raising a child in a dual-income or single-income household, time is scarce! Our time-deprive society has diminished the amount of attention most parents are able to provide their children. How then, do today's busy parents enhance the *quality* of attention they are capable of paying their child especially during their crucial developmental years—between the ages of three and six?

During this period, children acquire knowledge about themselves and the world around them, which begins to formulate their emotional and intellectual disposition. Parents should welcome this opportunity with great enthusiasm. In addition to planting the roots of a lifelong relationship, comes the pride and joy of knowing you are making them, and the world they live in, more valuable by taking the time to enhance the quality of their lives.

What a child learns during their early-age years will have an enormous influence upon the shape of their behavior as they grow up. These are their most formidable years. *If parents use their power to nourish their child's core qualities at an early age, they will maximize the chance that those qualities will become a positive force in their lives.*

> *The most important period of life is not the age of university studies, but the first one, the period from birth to the age of six.*
>
> —Maria Montessori

Whether having both a career and a family is a matter of necessity or desire, successful parenting begins and ends when you make your child's development your number one priority. I believe that parents can succeed on both work and family fronts in spite of the societal pressures stemming from our lifestyle changes. It can happen if parents use their power to incorporate sensible, consistent, and relevant parenting techniques into their daily routine.

I'm not suggesting that it's going to be easy . . . far from it! It's physically impossible for most parents to spend an abundance of time with their children. Therefore, *the solution lies not in our ability to expand the amount of time we spend with our kids, but by enhancing the quality of our interaction with them.* Accomplishing this goal for the sake of my own children motivated me to develop a wide assortment of **M**essages, **E**xercises, **A**ctivities, **L**essons, and **S**tories, hence the term, M.E.A.L.S., which would enhance the quality of time I spent with them.

Consider Kid M.E.A.L.S. another form of nutrition that you can add to your existing supply of healthy parenting practices. If they help a parent find only one extra way to spend quality time with their early-age child to enrich their heart and mind, it will be a step in the right direction.

Children will enjoy Kid M.E.A.L.S. because they are a fun and creative way to interact with Mom and Dad. Parents will love them because they are educational, easy-to-use, yet powerful techniques designed to enhance the quality of time, as limited as it may be, that you are able to devote to your child's personal development.

The Kid M.E.A.L.S. contained in *Parent Power* are designed to help parents nourish seven essential qualities vital to the healthy development of their child's emotional and intellectual foundation. If parents do everything they can to prepare their children for this amazing recipe we call life, then they must find a way to supply them with the proper ingredients early on. Taking the time to fortify their hearts and minds today makes it possible for them to live happy, rewarding, and fulfilled lives tomorrow.

Parents must make room in their hearts and then in their houses and then in their schedules for their children. No poor parent is too poor to do that and no middle-class parent is too busy.

—Jesse Jackson

KID M.E.A.L.S. OVERVIEW

Childhood is a place where people learn who they are and how to be that way.

—Jean Illsley Clark

OBJECTIVES

Parent Power **is not . . .**

- meant to "hurry up" the process of raising your early age child
- designed to build the "perfect child"
- a "quick fix" for busy parents looking for shortcuts to raising their child

Parent Power **is . . .**

- a valuable supply of positive ideas designed to nourish your child's emotional and intellectual development
- intended to supplement and reinforce your own parenting practices
- a method of enhancing the quality of time you spend with your child

PARENT POWER

There isn't a tool available that is more powerful and influential to a child's positive behavioral development than a parent's love and guidance.

Parents are the most persuasive figures in their child's life. That's why it's so important for them to be concerned about the quality of their interaction with them. Like any form of education, when serving Kid M.E.A.L.S. it's important to incorporate techniques that help make the quality of time you spend together meaningful. Here are four ingredients you should consider.

a) Listening

Unfortunately, most of us have never been taught to listen very well. It's natural for all of us to place our own feelings and beliefs before those of others—even when it comes to our own children. Effective parenting, however, requires good listening skills—the ability to get beyond hearing what you want to, and listen closely to the thoughts and emotions of your child. Your capability of listening, really listening, to your child and hear the things even they are not aware they are saying or feeling is extremely important in aiding them with their personal development. When a child's parent, whom they look up to with unspoken admiration, conveys their respect by listening to them, that parent strengthens the quality of their relationship with their child, as well as the relationship the child builds with themselves.

So, the next time your child tries to tell you something, even if it seems trite to you, respond in a way that lets them know you are really listening to them—establish eye contact, nod in agreement, or repeat back to them what they just said. This tells them you are listening.

b) Enthusiasm

The degree of enthusiasm you demonstrate toward your child, whether it's regarding a school project or on the soccer field, will have a significant impact on their behavior. An upbeat attitude is infectious and inspires their interest in whatever you focus their attention on. Therefore, your genuine enthusiasm in educational activities, such as those presented in the Kid M.E.A.L.S. series, will influence them to react in a similar fashion. This powerful parenting technique is the magic behind holding your child's interest in whatever it is you wish to teach them.

c) Conviction

Parents need to convey a sense of conviction in their actions, words, and deeds. The more conviction you put behind your behavior, the more meaningful its impact will be. An individual's conviction makes their behavior persuasive and believable. When your child believes that something is significant to you, then they silently register it as important to them. For example, if you emphasize, with conviction, your belief that *honesty* is valuable to you, then you will increase the propensity that your child will make *honesty* a part of their value system, too.

d) Praise and Encouragement

You have the power to influence your early-age child like no one else because they naturally want to please you. The more praise and encouragement you offer them, the more motivated they will be to continue demonstrating their abilities to you and, at the same time, build up confidence within themselves. It doesn't take long for a child to realize that meeting your expectations provides them with the love and attention they so strongly desire.

However, you must be sure to regulate the amount of praise you bestow upon your child. Showering them with too much is not healthy for their ego. This is a tricky proposition because there's a fine line between giving too much and too little. The objective is to make them feel good without going overboard. Or else, they will develop an over-inflated view of themselves. What's more, parents who constantly over-praise their children eventually make their own words and actions less believable. Be careful not to fall into this trap or your well-intentioned efforts will become counterproductive. Support them and encourage them, but be realistic.

DESIGN and FEATURES

The Kid M.E.A.L.S. series is presented in an easy to follow format. Each of the seven sections begins with a brief overview. They are then followed up by at least one **M**essage, **E**xercise, **A**ctivity, **L**esson, and **S**tory, hence **M.E.A.L.S.**, designed to support the nourishment of that particular quality within your child.

Messages appear at the beginning of each Kid **M.**E.A.L.S. section. This feature is designed to deliver valuable messages to your child. One type of message that you'll see frequently throughout the series comes in the form of either a WORD of the Day, QUESTION of the Day, or MOTTO of the Day. This type of message was designed to reach

KID M.E.A.L.S. OVERVIEW

and teach children in an efficient, yet effective manner—especially for working parents who can't be with their children during the week due to their work schedule.

Simply, leave a **M**essage on the table where your child eats breakfast. Briefly present it to them in the morning; and then, reference the same **M**essage later that evening, perhaps over dinner. Make sure the message sinks in, but make it an enjoyable part of your interaction with them so they'll respond to them in a positive way. Only engage your child with these types of messages once or twice a week. Saturating them with too many **M**essages will diminish their impact and effectiveness.

You'll see an Up-Link symbol placed next to designated Kids M.E.A.L.S.

It's a prompt that signals parents to reference the WORD of the Day, MOTTO of the Day, or QUESTION of the Day, later in the week, in an attempt to reinforce what you are trying to teach them.

The **M**essage feature within the Kid M.E.A.L.S. segments suggests a variety of ways to educate and inspire your child. But, don't only rely on the WORDS, MOTTOS, and QUESTIONS, presented in the series—create new ones which reflect the values and qualities you wish to teach them. I encourage you to use this portion of the Kid M.E.A.L.S. segments to communicate messages that *you* deem important based upon your own set of values.

Parent Power offers four other methods of nourishing essential qualities within your early age child. In addition to the **M**essage portion contained within each Kid M.E.A.L.S. section, you'll also find **E**xercises, **A**ctivities, **L**essons, and **S**tories which provide unique and creative ways to encourage the development of seven core areas of their personal development:

1. SELF-ESTEEM
2. EMOTIONAL DEVELOPMENT
3. COGNATIVE SKILLS
4. HONESTY
5. SELF-RELIANCE
6. CREATIVITY
7. PURPOSE

♦ Main Course ♦

♦ Chapter 1 ♦

"So, when he says, 'What a good boy am I,' Jack is really reinforcing his self-esteem."

SELF-ESTEEM

self•esteem, n.—worth; the quality that renders something valuable.

*Two lasting things you can give your child—one is wings,
the other is the desire to use them.*

—source unknown

You can use your power as a parent, in subtle as well as direct ways, to prepare your child's foundaton of self-esteem so they build confidence within themselves. Arthur Ash once said, "An important key to success is self-confidence . . . [and] an important key to self-confidence is preparation." Self-esteem, or confidence, is essential to the success of an individual's personal growth. Life is a challenging adventure. In order for your child to navigate their way through it, so they can live rich and rewarding lives, it's incumbent upon you, as their parent to do whatever you can to cultivate their self-esteem at an early age. Nourishing their confidence when they are young, on a small scale, prepares them to handle unavoidable challenges heading their way on a larger scale later in life.

The following "SELF-ESTEEM" Kid M.E.A.L.S. are designed to develop an early age child's foundation of confidence. Its future development will be cultivated from the quality of this soil. Therefore, it's necessary to nourish it with ingredients essential to its growth.

> *Self-worth comes from one thing—thinking that you are worthy.*
> *—Wayne Dyer*

Kid M.E.A.L.S.

SELF-ESTEEM — Message #1

[Age: 5+]

WORD of the Day

Happy

> The WORD of the Day, MOTTO of the Day, and QUESTION of the Day, feature appears throughout the **M**essage segment of the Kid M.E.A.L.S. series. As you'll come to see, this type of **M**essage is essentially a word or phrase expressing a positive **M**essage that you're interested in focusing your child's attention upon.
>
> The WORD, MOTTO, or QUESTION of the Day is designed to be left on the table where your child eats breakfast. Then, when you see them after work, ask them about the **M**essage you left behind in the morning—Discuss it briefly, and be enthusiastic about it, but do not dwell on it too much. Only engage them with these types of messages once or twice a week. Saturating them with too many will diminish their impact and effectiveness.

SELF-ESTEEM

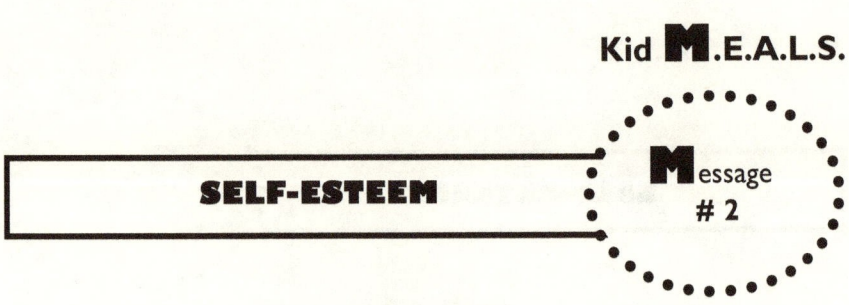

Uniquely Me

[Age 4-5] To reinforce your child's self-esteem and enhance their self-perception, here's a fun **M**essage to recite to them in front of a mirror.

What I See Is Uniquely Me

Mirror, mirror on the wall, what I see is uniquely me.
My eyes are (insert color of their eyes):   <u>blue</u>.
My hair is (insert color of their hair):   <u>brown</u>.
And I have (insert personal feature):   <u>freckles</u>, too.
Through thick and thin, till eternity,
What I see is uniquely me.

Kid M.E.A.L.S.

SELF-ESTEEM — **M**essage #3

Treasure Collection

[Age 3+] Send your child a **M**essage that makes them feel valuable. Build a file to collect all the arts and crafts they complete throughout their early-age years. Children feel great about their contributions when someone recognizes that what they've done is worth keeping. Label a folder "Treasure Collection" with your child's name on it, and place it somewhere that they can access it, too. When they complete a project they will know where to put it, so they can add to their collection.

The **M**essage you send your young child through the "Treasure Collection" project makes them feel and believe that who they are and what they do is valuable. They will take pride in knowing that there's a place where all their "stuff" worth saving can be found. Avoid bragging about their accomplishments, but make them feel good about what they've done so they recognize their own unique talents.

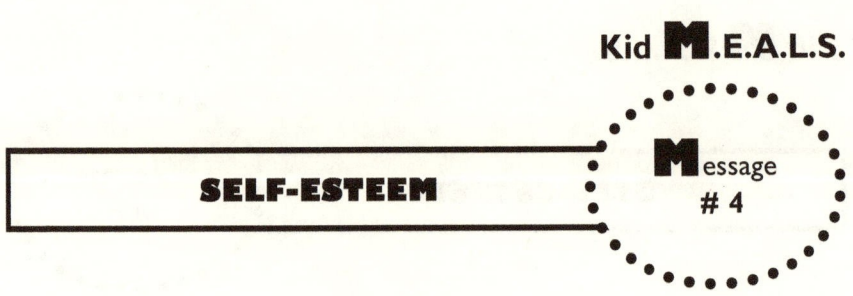

QUESTION of the Day

Who can make your dreams come true?

[Age 5-6] From time to time, all parents should encourage their child to pursue their hopes and dreams. It's a Message they will hear quite frequently when they are young. Their exposure to books, nursery rhymes, and movies may keep them silently wondering what this reference to "dreaming" is all about. They won't easily grasp the idea, but you can help them begin to understand that *they have* the power to make their "dreams" come true. As they get older, they will come to realize that they themselves have the ability to make their dreams come true.

When you arrive home from work in the evening, ask your child if they know what the QUESTION of the Day is. Then, ask them if they know the answer to the question. When they look to you for the answer, respond with a resounding, "YOU! That's right, it's YOU who has the power to make your dreams come true." Then, briefly explain that when they really want something, they shouldn't expect their dreams to magically come true just because hoped they would—that they have the power inside themselves to make their dreams a reality.

Up-Link
QUESTION of the Day

Who can make your dreams come true? (You!)

Kid M.E.A.L.S.

SELF-ESTEEM — **M**essage #5

Freedom to Fail

[Age 5+] When children associate mistakes or failure with negativity, they learn to avoid situations that can bring those types of feelings on. This **M**essage gives your child permission to make mistake, so they won't be discouraged by adversity, or build up fears that get in the way of their moving past failure. They listen to your words of encouragement and believe you, because they naturally trust you. When you unconditionally accept your child's efforts, they learn to identify success in terms of their effort, not just the outcome. Once you instill them with the permission, or freedom to fail, they will develop a willingness to take risks, even if it means failing.

When you find your child falling short of success, send them a **M**essage that communicates your desire to see them succeed, but places a greater emphasis on your admiration for their willingness to keep *trying*. For example, if they get upset because they've yet to score a goal in their soccer league, say, "Sure everyone wants to score a goal, but I know if you keep *trying* you're capable of scoring a goal . . . and even if you don't, I'm still very proud of you for *trying!*" This attitude encourages them to stay in the game even if they do not succeed at scoring a goal. The **M**essage emphasizes that it's just as important to do your best, and to keep trying, even when you fall short of your goals.

SELF-ESTEEM

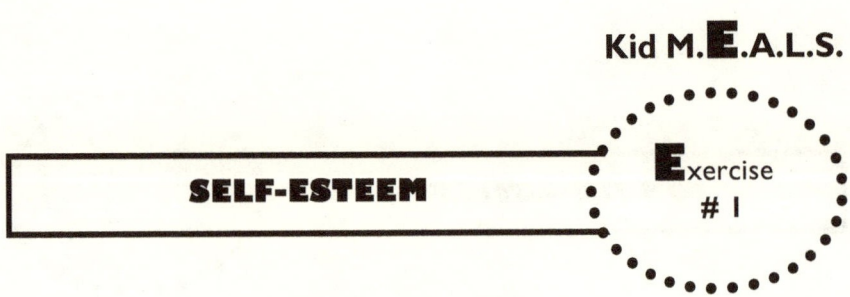

"Eye" Am Confident

[Age 5+] Children become confident when they learn to make eye contact while speaking with others. The "Eye Am Confident" Exercise begins to give kids the confidence to look someone directly in the eyes while they are speaking with them. Engaging in this Exercise encourages its development and emphasizes its value. It's best to perform it with a group of children. Many times when they see other kids act a certain way it encourages them to behave accordingly. If a child chooses not to participate, do not force them to stay in the game. Save it for a time when they feel a bit more comfortable, perhaps, in a one-on-one setting.

Gather a small group of kids and see which one can look you in the eyes the longest while speaking to you without blinking or looking away. While they are doing the Exercise have them repeat the saying, "I can look you in the eyes while talking to you without blinking," until they do. Whoever lasts the longest without blinking, wins! The best part of doing this Exercise with a group of kids is that someone always wants to challenge the winner. It could go on for a while. Try it and "Eye Am Confident" your child will become more comfortable looking people in the eyes while speaking.

Kid M.E.A.L.S.

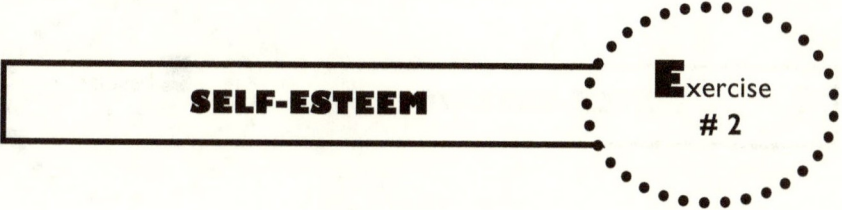

SELF-ESTEEM — Exercise #2

The Whole Picture

[Age 5+] This Exercise is designed to reveal to your child a balanced view of themselves, so they come to accept the areas in their life that need to be improved, without allowing the need for improvement to overshadow their positive qualities. It's important for parents to show their child, without over-inflating their ego, how to keep the positive side of their personality in view even though they will discover things that may not make them feel very good about themselves. Not losing sight of their positive attributes, will become an important part of your child's ability to accept themselves—even when others do not. This can happen when they are able to see the "whole picture."

Identify three things your child does well and three things your child would like to improve. Draw a box and write these qualities inside. When they are feeling down, remind them to see the "whole picture," so they don't develop a bad habit of always focusing too much on the negative side.

THE WHOLE PICTURE	
Jill **is**:	Jill **wants to improve**:
> Kind	> In sports
> Funny	> Not being so shy
> Smart	> Being sloppy

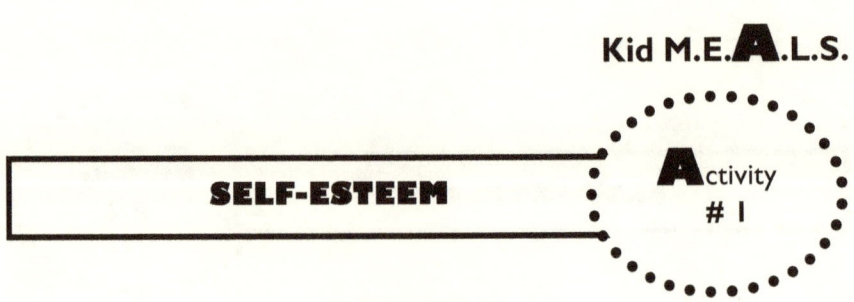

SELF-ESTEEM

Kidini Confidence

[Age 5+] Children feel good about themselves when they find the confidence to perform and communicate in front of others. Help them develop their verbal and non-verbal skills of communication by teaching them magic tricks and staging a show for friends and/or family.

Purchase a kid's magic book. Kids love magic tricks, and you can have a lot of fun showing them the secret to performing them. Once they learn how to perform a few tricks, they'll be eager to show others what they've learned. Without them even realizing it, they'll be building the confidence to express themselves in front of others. They won't feel like they're performing, they'll see this more as an Activity whereby they are "showing" others what they've learned. It's also fun to give your act a name, like "The Amazing Kidini and His Trusty Sidekick, Pop." Rehearse your act, and then take the show on the road. Whether it's after a dinner or at a family reunion, this Activity will nourish your child's self-esteem so they learn to feel comfortable expressing themselves in front of others.

Kid M.E.A.L.S.

SELF-ESTEEM — **A**ctivity #2

I Hear Me

[Age 4-6] Build your child's confidence and verbal skills by having fun with a tape recorder. They may act shy at first, but this **A**ctivity can help them overcome feelings of inadequacy, and you can have a lot of fun in the process.

Have your child speak into a tape recorder as they respond to questions from you about all sorts of things. Ask them about their favorite sports, games, or story characters. They may be looking forward to an upcoming event, such as a party, play date, or theme day at pre-school. Sing a nursery rhyme together, or perhaps you can create one of your own songs! Then, play it back to so they can hear themselves. This **A**ctivity builds their confidence to communicate outwardly while focusing on their positive qualities inside themselves.

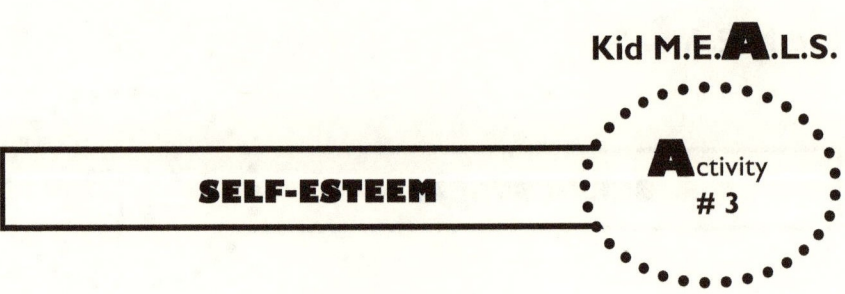

SELF-ESTEEM

Breaking News

[Age 4+] Get the video camera out and have fun playing television reporter. Create the scenario that your child is a firefighter and has just rescued the neighbor's cat from their tree in the backyard. Pretend you're a news reporter from a local television station, and you want to do a story to find out more about the hero behind the rescue. Make this **A**ctivity fun. During the interview, it's your job to learn as much about them as you can. You should listen carefully and be interested in your child's answers as they respond to your questions. Be enthusiastic about what they have to say—it will validate them and convey your appreciate about what they have to say. Here are some questions to get you started:

1. What do heroes like you do when you're not rescuing kittens?
2. You must really like your job. If you weren't a firefighter, what would you be?
3. Someone said that you also rescue rabbits and ferrets, it that true?

Have fun making them feel good about their answers and you'll build their confidence along the way.

Kid M.E.A.L.S.

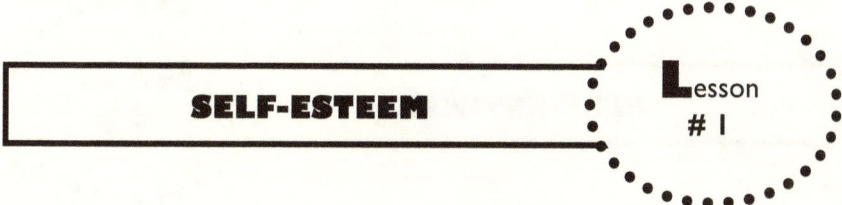

SELF-ESTEEM — Lesson #1

Domino Determination

[Age 6+] Whether it's striving to do well in school or learning how to play basketball, along the way it takes self-esteem to get past the rough spots. This **Lesson** teaches your child that reaching goals requires the confidence and determination to *keep going* especially when you encounter set backs along the way. It's designed to encourage them to keep trying, just in case they don't succeed the first time. You'll need a set of dominos to demonstrate this **Lesson**.

A great time to teach them this **Lesson** is just before they begin learning how to ride a two-wheel bike. Explain to them that it may seem too difficult learning how to ride a two-wheel bike, and they may even fall down . . . but if they get back up and continue to try, eventually they'll reach their goal. Before heading outside to teach them how to ride a two-wheel bike, take the time to teach them that getting back up if they fall down gets them one step closer to reaching their goal.

Line up a set of dominos on the kitchen floor leaving two gaps in the line—one near the middle and the other toward the end. Then, have your child tip the first domino over in an attempt to knock all of them down. When the dominos stop falling at the first gap you made in the middle, explain to them that just because it stopped doesn't mean that it's not possible to reach the end . . . it just means that you must continue where they stopped falling and start again from that point. Have them push the next standing domino, and watch them fall, until it catches up to the last gap. At this point in the **Lesson**, explain that when they are learning how to ride a two-wheel bike for the first time, sometimes they may fall down . . . Falling down doesn't mean that you can't do it; it just means that you have to get back up and try again. Success may only be a step away . . . just like it will be with this line of dominos. Watch what happens when we try to get to the end of the domino line with just one more try.

Then, push the next domino over, and watch as the remainder of them fall down. Conclude the **L**esson by reminding your child that even when they fall down, having the determination to keep trying is what will make it possible for them to get back up until they reach their goals.

Kid M.E.A.L.S.

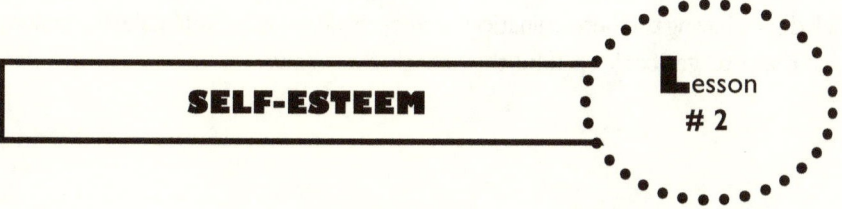

SELF-ESTEEM — Lesson #2

Com-Pear

[Age 4+] Early on, your child will compare themselves to other children. They'll silently wonder if they are supposed to be more like their friends, or if their friends are supposed to be more like them. To illustrate the point that everyone is unique and special in their own way and that we should learn to accept ourselves in spite of these differences, engage them in the Com-Pear Lesson.

Take two or three fruit pairs and slice them down the middle, not top to bottom, but sideways. The center design on each side of the pear will look the same. Before doing so reveal to your child the differences between the two or three pairs on the outside (note the color, shape, size, condition, etc.). Then demonstrate after slicing the pairs in half that regardless of their outer appearance, all pairs look the same inside. Explain that people are just like the pairs. They differ in how they look and act on the outside, but inside they all have the same unique design. And just like the seeds in the center make the pairs grow and blossom to their own full potential, likewise, each person has the same uniqueness waiting to be developed inside themselves, too.

Kid M.E.A.L.S.

SELF-ESTEEM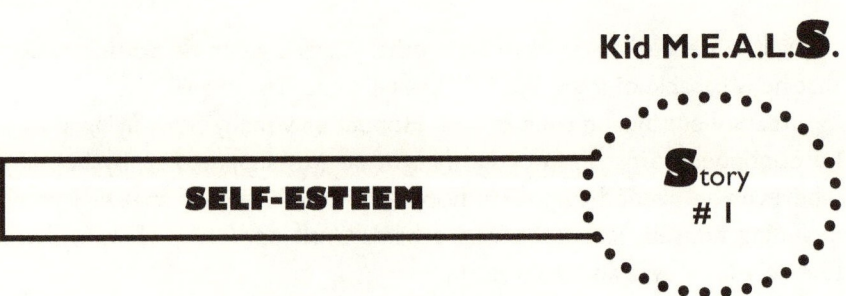

Story #1

A Change of View Helped Hopper Soar

[Age 4+] This **S**tory illustrates how a little bird, named Hopper, found the courage to discover his true nature.

One day Willie the Worm woke up and crawled out of his tiny earth hole in Shane's (substitute with your child's name) backyard to meet a beautiful new day. His friend, Rachael the Rabbit was waiting for him to come out and play. As he looked up at her he noticed a baby bird bending over the edge of its nest in the tree top above her head. The tiny bird must have just been born and was left all alone inside its nest while its mother went out looking for some food. Weak and uncertain of himself, the newborn accidentally stumbled out of his nest landing just a few feet away from Willie. Willie made his way over to the bird, and to his delight the bird seemed unharmed. Just then, Willie's good friend Rachael the Rabbit, hopped over to see what was going on. They quickly became friends and began playing together in the backyard.

Rachael and Willie realized that their new friend needed a name, so they decided to call him Hopper. Willie came up with the name, because it reminded him of how the bird leapt out of his nest when they first met and "hopped" around like Rachael the Rabbit. Eventually, he thought to himself, Hopper will learn to fly just like other birds. But as you'll come to see, that was not going to happen any time soon.

A few days later when Willie saw Rachael he asked her what happened to Hopper. She told him that Hopper's mom never came back to the nest so she took him back to her house where she and her family could look after him. Eventually, Hopper became a member of Rachael the Rabbit's family. Hopper enjoyed growing up with Rachael and her entire family of rabbits. Then one day it occurred to Willie, while he was playing with Hopper, that he'd never seen him fly. The only way Hopper ever got around was like Rachael the Rabbit and the rest of her family—by hopping. Oh well, Willie thought, since he's never been with other birds, I guess he doesn't realize that he is capable of flying, but I wonder if some day he will?

Years went by, and even though Hopper saw many birds flying above, he continued to *act the way he thought he was supposed to*, by hopping wherever he needed to go. He hopped around so much that everyone, including himself, forgot he was a bird. Until one chilly morning, just before winter was about to set in.

Hopper was standing at the foot of the Shane's swing set in the backyard when a bird that looked just like him flew into the yard and landed by his side. The bird told Hopper that he and his friends were flying south for the winter. He asked Hopper if he wanted to join them. A bit confused, Hopper exclaimed, "But I can't fly." The other bird said, "Sure you can . . . you're a bird." Hopper responded, "If I am, then why can't I fly?" "Have you ever tried?" asked the other bird. "No," said Hopper. As he paused to reflect on his answer, he thought to himself, "I guess it's because I never tried to?" The other bird announced proudly, "It's easy, watch me, all you need to do is flap your wings like this."

Off he went to the top of the swing set. Once he got there, he yelled down at Hopper, "Now you try it!" But he wasn't confident that he could do it. However, the one thing Hopper didn't lack was courage. So, he mustered up as much as he could; he spread his wing out as far as possible, took a deep breath, and said to himself with a reassuring tone, "I can fly, I know I can . . . I'm a bird and birds were meant to fly." At that moment Hopper thrust himself into the air toward the top of the swing set. He began flapping his wing furiously and was determined give it all he had in order to make it to the top. Suddenly he felt himself getting lighter, and for a few seconds he actually believed that he was going to make it. Except he only made it halfway there. Suddenly he came tumbling back to the earth. As he dusted himself off, he believed for the first time in his life that maybe he really could fly. Even though he failed to make it the first time, he found the courage to try once again, because deep down he believed it was possible.

It was then that he recognized that he was capable of flying like the bird that he was, even though after all these years he only knew how to hop around like a rabbit. Looking up at the other bird, Hopper remarked, "Here I come!" On that day, he experienced the greatest feeling of his life. He discovered that acting like a rabbit was hiding who he really was— a bird, not a rabbit.

Launching himself into the air, he began to soar to the top of Shane's swing set, until he landed next to the other bird. He looked down into the backyard and for the first time saw it from a view he'd never seen before. From that day on, his view of himself also changed—all because he had the courage to discover his true nature.

Kid M.E.A.L.S.

SELF-ESTEEM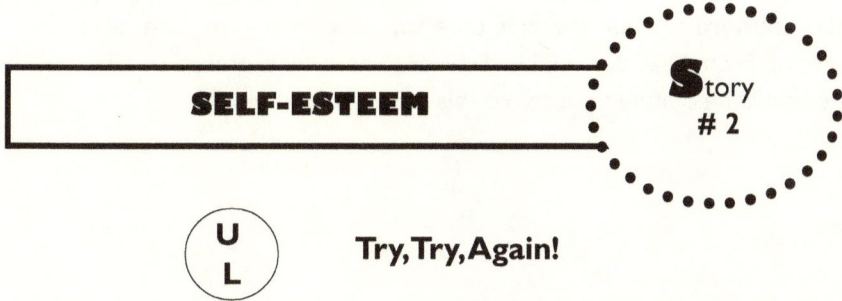

(U L) **Try, Try, Again!**

[Age 3-5] Willie the Worm and his friend, Sammy the Squirrel, were in Shane's (substitute with your child's name) backyard one afternoon looking for chestnuts. There were plenty high atop the trees, however, Willie was too small to make it to the top of a chestnut tree, so he asked Sammy if he'd climb up to get a few. As much as Sammy wanted them, he hesitated because he was afraid he would fall from the tree on his way up. However, Sammy was very motivated to try because he was also hungry and loved chestnuts just as much as Willie! With a little encouragement, Willie was able to convince Sammy to give it a try. But Sammy didn't make it very far up the tree because, as he feared, he slipped and fell back to the ground. Yet, Sammy's courage wouldn't allow him to give up. He brushed himself off and looked at Willie with determination. Willie looked back at him and said, "If at first you don't succeed Sammy, try, try again," which is exactly what he did. This time, he made it all the way to the top inches away from the chestnuts which were hanging on the end of the branch. "You can do it, Sammy, I know you can . . . just be careful," Willie yelled. He stepped out on to the limb and was successful knocking a whole bunch off the tree to the ground where Willie collected them. When Sammy came down, Willie thanked him and said, "I'm proud of you, Sammy, you never gave up. You had the courage to get back up even after you fell. If you hadn't kept trying, we would still be hungry."

Up-Link
<u>MOTTO of the Day</u>

If at first you don't succeed—try, try, again !

Kid M.E.A.L.**S**.

SELF-ESTEEM → **S**tory # 3

A Head Start Down the Yellow Brick Road

[Age 4+] You can make the age-old tale, *Wizzard of Oz*, more interesting and meaningful to your child simply by inserting them into the **S**tory. It's a great way to instill them with the **S**tories message regarding the value of believing in one's self. If you're not familiar with the *Wizard of Oz* **S**tory, then watch or read it. Then, use it as backdrop to customizing your own version that includes your child.

Set your child up to be the **S**tory central figure, Dorothy, who's trying to find her way back *home*. In your child's adventure through the land of Oz they'll encounter three character, the Scarecrow, Tin Man, and Lion, each in searching for something, as well. The Scarecrow is looking for a *brain*; the Tin Man is looking for a *heart*; and the Lion is looking for *courage*. Their search down the yellow brick road leads them to ultimately realize that what they are looking for has always been inside themselves.

I can assure you that even parents will keep their child's attention, because they love to hear **S**tories that include themselves in the action. Just think how attentive he or she will be when they watch or read the original version of *Oz*. They'll already know that the answer to what Dorothy (or in this case, your child), is looking for can be found not outside themselves, but inside.

Chapter 2

"Today we're going to explore in paint how we feel when we're picked up late from preschool."

EMOTIONAL DEVELOPMENT

e•mo•tion, *n.*—a mental state that arises spontaneously rather than through conscious effort.

*Your emotions affect every cell in your body.
Mind, body, mental and physical, are all intertwined.*

—*Thomas Tutko*

Emotions are extremely powerful. Therefore, paying attention to how they impact your child's personal development at an early age is vital to their ability to understand them as they grow up. That's why it is equally important for parents to cultivate their child's heart, as much as their mind. This is perhaps the most powerful contribution you can make toward preparing them for a successful journey through life.

As complex as children are, it is still possible for parents to develop their emotional awareness at an early age. I'm not suggesting that you overload them with excess emotional baggage, however, raising kids does require a willingness to teach them how to communicate what they are feeling to themselves, as well as others. The "EMOTIONAL DEVELOPMENT" Kid M.E.A.L.S. are designed to help you accomplish this goal.

Kid M.E.A.L.S.

EMOTIONAL DEVELOPMENT — Message #1

WORD of the Day

Listen

[Parents] Acknowledging what your child has to say is vital to their emotional development. When you take time to really listen to your child, it validates their feelings, thus who they are becomes meaningful. So, this WORD of the Day needs to be directed toward you—their parent.

Note: Take time to think about the power of this word as you go through your own day. Pay attention to how well you are listening and, how well those around you listen to what you have to say. Recognize your own limitations and resolve to turn your listening skills around, until it becomes a habit that spills over into all of your relationships.

Kid M.E.A.L.S.

EMOTIONAL DEVELOPMENT

Message #2

[Age: 3+]

WORD(s) of the Day

I love you

In some families, these words come easily. But if you never heard them growing up, you may not feel comfortable using them. It may feel unnatural to you. However, using words that express affection should not be relegated just for special moments. Your child needs to hear, and see, these words often. Don't just assume they know you love and care about them. Positive words of expression are powerful sources of nourishment for your child's heart to grow on. When they become a regular part of your vocabulary, your children become comfortable expressing themselves with positive emotional words, too.

Make it a point to send your child a written breakfast **Message** such as the one above. But also get accustomed to verbalizing messages that communicate to your child how much you love and care about them.

Kid **M**.E.A.L.S.

EMOTIONAL DEVELOPMENT

Message #3

Humor—nature's medicine

[Age 4-6] Send your child a **M**essage that conveys the value of humor in their lives. People who can laugh at themselves and life enrich the quality of their relationship with themselves, and with others, because it helps them relax and enjoy life.

There are a lot of ways to communicate the value of humor to your child. Make "joke time" a priority in your family. At least once a week tell your child a joke. Encourage them to tell them to friends and relatives. Make humor a part of their lives. The most effective way you can instill your child with a sense of humor is by frequently letting them see that side of you.

> Knock knock
> Who's there?
> Noah.
> Noah who?
> Noah good place to find more jokes?

EMOTIONAL DEVELOPMENT

Kid M.E.A.L.S.

Message #4

Relax and Have Fun

[Age 5+] If you know your child is about to take on a challenging task, such as a spelling test or soccer game, leave them the following Message poem to encourage them to relax and have fun. Here's a sample (replace the name on the top line with your child's; and the subject of interest on the line within the body of the poem).

<u>Shane,</u>
Good things are sure to come your way.
So smile when you (<u>*take your test*</u>) today.
Relaxing makes it feel more fun.
that is when you know you've really won!

Kid M.E.A.L.S.

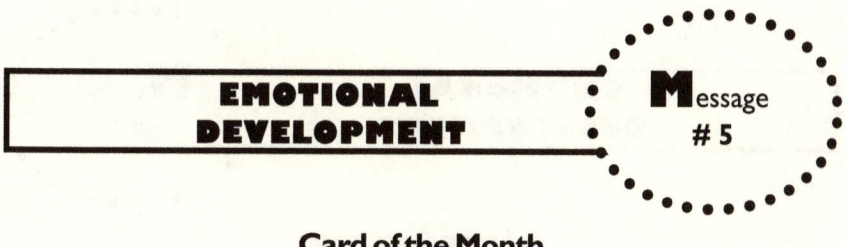

EMOTIONAL DEVELOPMENT — Message #5

Card of the Month

[Age 3+] From your office, mail your child a card that tells them that you love them.

EMOTIONAL DEVELOPMENT

Exercise #1

Sixty-Second Stress Reducer

[Age 5+] It only takes sixty seconds to teach your child an effective way of dealing with emotional stress through the "Sixty-Second Stress Reducer" Exercise. When you notice your child becoming emotionally strained, help them ease the burden and learn how to calm down. Lightly massage their shoulders or palms while you quietly count down from sixty. Tell them to take deep breaths in the process. When there are ten seconds remaining, stop massaging them and place your hands in one spot until the Exercise winds down. It takes a minute of love and care to demonstrate this simple technique to your child. It may not take all the stress away, but it lets them know that their emotions are important, and they need to be addressed. Being involved also brings you closer to them at a time when they require your compassion, wisdom, and affection.

Kid M.E.A.L.S.

EMOTIONAL DEVELOPMENT

Exercise #2

Fun in the Dark

[Age: 4+] This Exercise helps diminish your child's fear of the dark. Just before bedtime, announce that you're going to play "camp out." You'll need a flashlight. Jump into bed with your child while the lights in the room are *still on*. Now, turn the flashlight on and proceed to point the beam of light at all the different objects in their room (toys, stuffed animals, balls, etc.). Then let your child be the one who gets up, turns out the lights using the flashlight, and makes their way back into bed. Lie in in bed with them and let them wander around the room with the flashlight beam and have some fun. Ask if you can have a turn, then begin pointing out all the things in your child's room. Hand the flashlight back to them, and ask them if they'd like to play a game. With the flashlight still on, turn the bedroom lights off. While they are pointing to one of the objects in the room with the flashlight beam, ask them if they think the object they are pointing the beam onto will still be there when you turn the flashlight off, then on again. Assure them that it will. Then ask them to turn the flashlight off so you can prove your point. Wait a second, then have them turn the flashlight back on to see that the ball is still there. Say, with calm confidence, "See it's still there!" Ask your child to pick out other objects in the room and keep doing the same Exercise, but increase the amount of time that the flashlight is turned off. Once they becomecomfortable with the darkness, their fears are sure to fade away.

EMOTIONAL DEVELOPMENT

Exercise #3

Guess Sketch

[Age: 4-6] Learning the value of relaxation is important in a person's life. Teach your child how to enjoy relaxing. There will be plenty of times throughout their lives when they'll need an emotional breather or simply need to calm down. The following Exercise helps channels your child's energy toward a calm and peaceful zone. A great time to perform this Exercise is when your child is having a difficult time calming down before bedtime. Announce that as soon as they get in bed you'll play "Guess Sketch." Once they climb into bed ask them to hold out one of their hands, palm facing up, so you can begin. Stretch their palm out and pass yours on top of it several times like you're smoothing it out. With your palm on top of theirs, ask them to shut their eyes, clear their mind, and have them take three deep breaths. Next, let them know that you're going to erase the sketch board so you can clear their mind before you begin. The object of the Exercise is to trace shapes and/or figures on their palm until they guess what you have sketched. Your child will have quieted down by now as they prepare to guess what you are going to draw on their palm. If your child is under four years of age, you may want to sketch shapes (circles, squares, triangles, etc.), which are relatively easy for them to recognize. If they are older, then advance the Exercise to include impressions of numbers or letters. This Exercise can also be done on your child's back.

Kid M.E.A.L.S.

EMOTIONAL DEVELOPMENT — **Exercise #4**

(U L) **Want What You Need**

[Age 6+] A proactive way of getting your children to focus on being satisfied with what they *have* as opposed to being unhappy about what they do not have—but *want*—is to talk to them about the difference between the two in a context that's easy for them to grasp. Wait for your child to ask for something they really don't need, such as a new bike, then engage them with the following Exercise.

Phase 1: Shane (substitute with your child's name), there are things that you *need*, and other things that you *want*. If you don't get some of the things you want that's okay . . . as long as you have what you *need*. Let me explain what I mean. You and I *need* (emphasize the word "need") food, for example, to stay alive, correct? Here's another example, you and I *need* a house to sleep in and protect us from bad weather . . . Food and a house are examples of things we *need* (emphasize the word "need"). Shane, do you agree that we *need* food to eat and a house to live in? When they respond yes, ask them to repeat for you what it is they *need*. Then, follow up with the following statement in a casual tone, "You're such a good learner . . . that's one of the things I love about you!"

Phase 2: Now let's try this one . . . not only do we need things, we *want* (emphasize the word "want") things too! Are there things you *want*? For instance, you said that you *wanted* a new bike, am I right? Extend the Exercise to include something else they might want, such as a new set of crayons. Repeat back to them the two items they *want* in the following manner, "So you *want* a new set of crayons, and you *want* a new bike, correct?" Don't move on with the Exercise until they are able to acknowledging what you said by verbalizing what the two items are that they *want*. Once they do, praise them again for being so bright.

Phase 3: Go back and refer to phase 1. Ask them to give you an example of something they *need*. Praise them when they get it correct. Then ask them to name something they *want*. Praise them again for being so smart. By now, the two concepts should be in place for you to make the distinction between them. If it doesn't set in right away, don't grow impatient. Step away from it and come back to it another time. You don't want to overwhelm your child. If they pick up on it the first time around, continue the Exercise by saying, "Okay lets see if you know the difference between what you *need* and what you *want*." With a hint of laughter in your voice say, "You don't *need a bike*, do you?" If they say yes, correct them and remind them that they don't *need* a bike . . ." You *need* food in order to stay alive, explain, and you *need* a house to protect you from bad whether, but you don't *need* a bike . . . you *want* a bike. Let's try it again, do you *need* a bike?" For the Exercise to be successful, they must agree that they don't *need* a bike. "If you don't have a bike is it impossible to live? Of course not, but if you didn't have food you would starve, wouldn't you? You see you don't *need* a bike, you *want* a bike." Get their attention and finish the Exercise by asking, "Getting what you *need* is more important than getting what you *want*, isn't that right Shane?"

As complicated as this Exercise may seem, you'll be surprised at how your child will be able to grasp its meaning.

Up-Link
<u>MOTTO of the Day</u>

Want what you need!

Kid M.E.A.L.S.

EMOTIONAL DEVELOPMENT

Exercise #5

Lift the Weight of Blame With Forgiveness

[Age: 5+] When life doesn't go our way, we direct blame about the situation toward ourselves or others as a way of rationalizing the pain or disappointment we are experiencing. Learning the value of forgiveness will teach your child to forgive others, as well as themselves. The following Exercise demonstrates how forgiveness will enable them to let go and let up on themselves and others.

Whenever your child experiences something that causes them emotional pain or disappointment, have them place a marble inside a small cup. Each marble represents an event that caused them to think poorly about themselves or someone else. For instance, they may fail a test at school or lose a baseball game because of their strikeout and blame themselves. Or, they miss the school bus and blame the bus driver for leaving without them. How they choose to communicate their dissatisfaction with themselves and others will have an effect on how they and others end up feeling about the situation at hand. After you've collected enough marbles to weigh the cup down, place it in a shallow bowl of water. With the cup weighed down to the bottom explain to your child that the weight of the marbles inside the cup are just like the weight of blame that will build up inside them if they focus too much on blaming others, or themselves, when they feel that life has treated them unfairly. Remind them that everyone makes mistakes. Further explain that when they allow those mistakes and errors to build up blame inside themselves, it means that they then must carry around excess weight that will hold them down much like the cup sitting at the bottom of the bowl. The only way to lift this weight which builds up inside us is through forgiveness. It's important to admit how you feel, but if you don't forgive yourself and others you will only build up more disappointment. When we forgive, it's like taking the marbles out or the cup. Look what happens when we do that. Notice that the cup begins to lighten up and float back to the top. The cup wants to come to the surface. It's natural tendency is to float, just as your natural tendency is to be happy. But that's not possible when you allow blame to hold you down. Forgiveness is like taking the marbles out of the cup so you can lighten the load and feel better about yourself and others.

Kid M.E.A.L.S.

EMOTIONAL DEVELOPMENT

Kid Compassion

[Age 4+] When we teach our children the value of care and compassion, we help them develop empathy toward others. Acts of kindness and charity will enhance your child's understanding of how fortunate they are, and at the same time, teach them the value of compassion by reaching out and helping those who are less fortunate than themselves.

Express empathy toward people outside your family circle with the following charitable Activity. Around the holidays go out of your way to pick up an extra gift(s) for a child or family at a local homeless shelter. Your child will be shy about giving the gift to another child they don't even know, so keep the act of kindness simple. Wrap the gift with your child and write on a blank card, "To someone special, from someone who cares." Call an area homeless shelter and ask them for the name of a child, or family, whom you can extend a gift(s) to (Be sure to check with the shelter beforehand to see if they have any gift giving policies). Then, deliver the gift(s) with your child to the homeless shelter. If your child is feeling particularly bold, then go out of your way to present the gifts to them personally. Or, you can just leave them at the front desk at the reception area. Either way, you are taking a positive step toward demonstrating the meaning of compassion and empathy.

EMOTIONAL DEVELOPMENT

Lesson #1

Show of Affection

[Age 4+] Demonstrating your ability and willingness to express your emotions toward others, especially your spouse, is healthy and natural. Withholding or suppressing feelings of affection inhibits your child's chances of ever learning about the value of these gestures, because it's simply not a subject that is taught outside the home. Therefore, make it your responsibility, as their parent, to display appropriate forms of affection in front of your child. This is a better way to nourish your child's emotional development than relying on someone else in society to demonstrate such values.

Moderate forms of affection, such as giving your spouse a kiss on the cheek, holding hands, and using affectionate terms in front of your child teach them the **L**esson that gestures of affection are a healthy form of behavior. Don't hesitate to express your feelings of affection toward your children either. Hug them, kiss them, and don't be shy about telling them you love them every day.

Kid M.E.A.L.S.

EMOTIONAL DEVELOPMENT — Lesson #2

Nature Walk

[Age 6+] The best Lessons we can discover about how to cope with our problems is learning how to relax. Hopefully, your child will not have to deal with severe problems as a young child. But in the event that they do, like losing a close relative or witnessing something traumatic, guiding them through the emotional setback will be an important step in their emotional development. Before such a situation occurs, introduce them to one of the most natural forms of relaxation—the power of nature.

Spend time with your child outdoors at a park, or even in the mountains, shows them a place where they can be a part of something bigger than their immediate surroundings. It gives them a perspective that is open, fresh, peaceful, and calm. It takes them away from their normal routine and expands their universe. The next time you're having a bad day, teach your child a Lesson about how a simple walk outdoors can be a healthy emotional outlet. Take them for a walk through your Local Park and show them how to focus on nature's wonders instead of life's disappointments.

Kid M.E.A.L.S.

EMOTIONAL DEVELOPMENT

Story #1

Dumb Words

[Age 5+] One day, Willie the Worm was playing with his friends, Rachael the Rabbit and Rocky the Raccoon, in Shane's (substitute with your child's name) sandbox in the backyard. Everyone was having a lot of fun, so the **S**tory goes, until Rocky and Rachael began bickering over who was going to use the shovel and pale. The two argued so much that it turned into a battle of teasing and name-calling. Rocky became so angry and frustrated that he lost control of himself and began using language that was not very nice—or smart—to let Rachael know how he felt.

Willie's dad was in the backyard at the time, and he overheard what was going on. He came over and asked Rocky and Rachael to make up. Then, he told them that Willie needed to go home for lunch. On the way back home, Willie's dad told him that some of the words he heard Rocky use weren't very nice. He explained that the reason he used them was because he wasn't able to explain what he was feeling inside. "You see, Willie, it's harder to use smart words to explain what you're feeling than it is to use dumb words ... because it takes more effort, intelligence, and patience. If you're smart, you don't need to use dumb words like the ones you heard Rocky use today. Using curse words to let someone know how you feel is dumb. Be smart, Willie, and don't ever start!"

Kid M.E.A.L.S.

EMOTIONAL DEVELOPMENT

Story #2

Willie the Worm's Focus on Feelings

[Age 5+] Emotions that do not make your child feel very good about themselves come in many forms. Whether it's embarrassment, sadness, or failure, there are many types of emotions that are bound to upset your child. Helping them understand that these emotions are a normal part of life helps ease the pain when they experience negative events. Share the following **S**tory with them, and perhaps the next time your child has difficulty getting beyond an emotional setback, it will help them address their feelings.

Willie the Worm couldn't wait to play soccer with the other kids in the neighborhood. During the weekends in the fall, everyone would show up in Shane's (substitute with your child's name) backyard for Saturday soccer. When Willie and several of his other friends showed up for the first game, Rocco the Raccoon noticed that Sammy the Squirrel had a hole in one of his sneakers, and he began to tease him, saying, "Cover the hole in your sneaker, Sammy, then maybe the rest of us won't have to smell your stinky feet." Everyone looked down at the hole in Sammy's sneaker and began laughing at him. Rocco's comment made Sammy feel very bad. All the laughter embarrassed him so much that he almost began to cry. Willie noticed how it made his friend Sammy feel, so he quickly interrupted all the laughter and shouted, "Let's get on with the game."

Sammy kept thinking that all the other kids were staring at the hole in his sneaker—but they weren't. Willie remembered what it felt like when he got embarrassed once, so he pulled his friend aside and said, "Sammy, don't let Rocco get to you. Go out there and show these guys what those sneakers are really made of!" Willie knew how Sammy felt, and that made Sammy feel a little bit better. He thought to himself, Willie is right, perhaps I am making a bigger deal than I should out of this. That's when he decided not to dwell on his bad feelings. It occurred to him that if he continued to feel bad it wouldn't make him feel any better, only worse. So he sprung to his feet and ran out on to the field, yelling, "Look out, here comes stinky feet." His embarrassment soon went away when the first person to score a point was ol' "Stinky Feet!"

◆ Chapter 3 ◆

"We've got enough rocks—what we need is better intelligence."

COGNITIVE SKILLS

cog•ni•tive, *adj.*—aware; attentive; knowledgeable.

A child uneducated is a child lost.

—John F. Kennedy

Nourishing your child's cognitive skills is vital to their intellectual well-being. If parents expect their child to succeed academically, they must use their power to foster intellectual confidence within them at an early age. You shouldn't expect them to speak three languages or calculate mathematic formulas by the age of six, however teaching them basic cognitive skills will get them off to a good start. This will maximize their chance of meeting the educational challenges that lie ahead of them.

No one is better equipped than a parent to nourish the cognitive skills of their pre-school child. Working hand-in-hand with educators, as they grow up, will maintain and strengthen their academic performance. I'm not suggesting that you over-develop your child academically. If you push them beyond their normal stage of development, they may become bored or worse yet feel out of place.

If you use each academic accomplishment to further build their confidence and nourish their intellectual appetite, you will make them come back for more. When education is fun and informative, it feels good; and when it feels good, your child's thirst for knowledge will grow. The "COGNITITVE SKILLS" Kid M.E.A.L.S. provide parents with tools to help them achieve this goal.

Kid M.E.A.L.S.

COGNITIVE SKILLS — Message #1

Message(s) of the DAY

(Examples, by age group)

[Age 3-4] LETTER of the Day

A

(Choose a different letter each day of the week)

NUMBER of the Day

3

(Choose a different number each day of the week)

[Age 4-5] WORD of the Day

Fun

NUMBER of the Day

20

[Age 5-6] WORD(s) of the Day

Friends share

QUESTION of the Day

5 + 5 = ____

COGNITIVE SKILLS

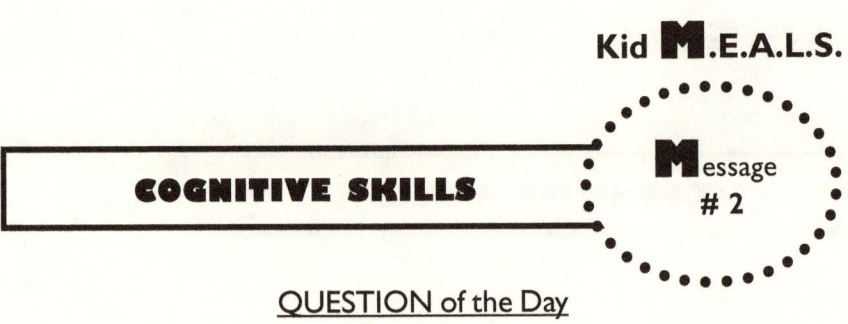

QUESTION of the Day

[Age 3-4] Leave behind a written question for them to answer that challenges their knowledge and increases their academic awareness in whatever subject you choose. It's a simple and effective way to stimulate their intellectual development. You will build your child's interest in these questions by reacting with enthusiasm and excitement after they've completed them.

Follow up on the question later that day. Make them feel good about their answer. If their answer was incorrect, take the opportunity to guide them in the right direction—stay positive and upbeat.

Here's a sample:

> If you have 2 apples in a basket and you add 1 orange to the basket, how many pieces of fruit are now in the basket?
>
> **What does 2+1= _____ ?**

Kid M.E.A.L.S.

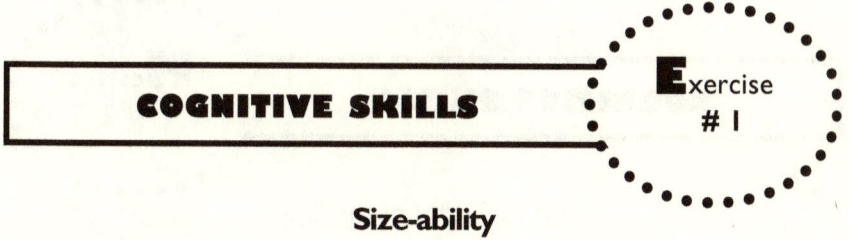

COGNITIVE SKILLS — Exercise #1

Size-ability

[Age 3-4] While sitting in any room in your house, ask your child the following types of questions to get them to think about spacial and size differences:

1) Which is closer, the bathroom or the backyard?
2) Which is farther, the playground or your playroom?
3) Which is bigger, your bedroom or the house?
4) Which is smaller, a marble or a beach ball?

COGNITIVE SKILLS

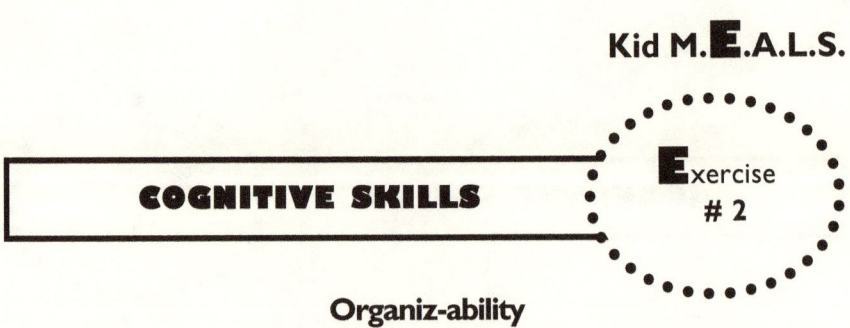

Organiz-ability

[Age 4-6] Teach your child how to organize the little things in life, and the big things will have a better chance of falling into place later on.

The evening before pre-school or kindergarten, have them participate in organizing their school bag. Have them collect any books, papers, or supplies that they may need for school the following day. Also, let them prepare the items that will go into their lunch box. Resist the temptation to do it for them because you're too busy to wait for them to do it themselves, or else you will rob them of the opportunity to develop their "organiz-ability."

Kid M.E.A.L.S.

COGNITIVE SKILLS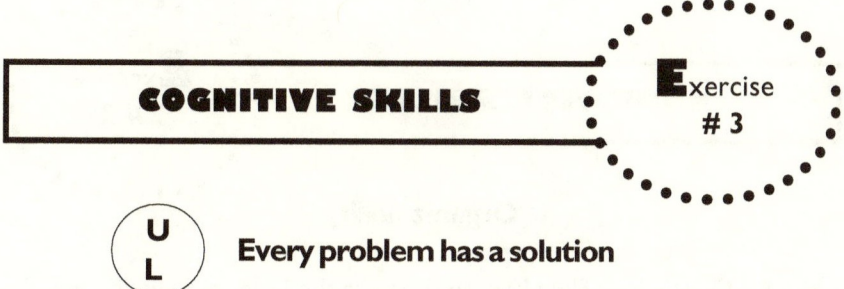

Exercise #3

U L — **Every problem has a solution**

[Age 3-4] Having the ability and enthusiasm to solve problems will become a vital asset in the life of your child. "Solution thinking" will come into play every day of their lives. By injecting a positive attitude into the process, you will increase their propensity to make this a positive part of how they learn to take on those challenges. Unless they develop a healthy attitude about solving problems, whether it's academic, social, or personal, the process will be perceived as a burden rather than a challenge they welcome. This **E**xercise helps your child develop an attitude that problems are less a burden and more a way of life.

Here's how it works. Leave the backdoor of your house open and lock the front one. Standing with your child outside the locked front door, explain to them that you just encountered a problem. Tell them the problem is that you can't get past the front door because it is locked from the inside, and you need their help to *solve* the problem. They'll want to help you out, but you need to inform them that you need a *solution*. Then, announce with excitement that you've found one. *Explain* to them that they need to run around and come thru the backdoor and unlock the front door in order to *solve the problem*. When they meet you at the front door, greet them with great enthusiasm as though they just discovered a new toy. At this point, be excited that they helped you find a *solution to the problem* . . . Let them know that without their help you wouldn't have been able to find a *solution*. Now comes the most important part of the **E**xercise. Convey to your child that every problem, like this one, has a *solution*. Have them recite that statement back to you. Then, repeat the entire **E**xercise once more, so it sinks in.

Before completing the **E**xercise, ask them pointedly, "What does every problem have?" They'll tell you—a solution. Congratulate them for understanding the point of the **E**xercise. Lastly, when your child goes to bed that evening, ask them to tell you again what every problem has. Days later, you may want to comment in front of your child to your spouse that Billy (substitute with your child's name) knows that there's a solution to every problem. In the future, when you ask them to find a solution, remember to keep it playful so it discourages them from perceiving problem solving as a burden.

Up-Link
QUESTION of the Day

What does every problem have? (A solution!)

Kid M.E.A.L.S.

COGNITIVE SKILLS

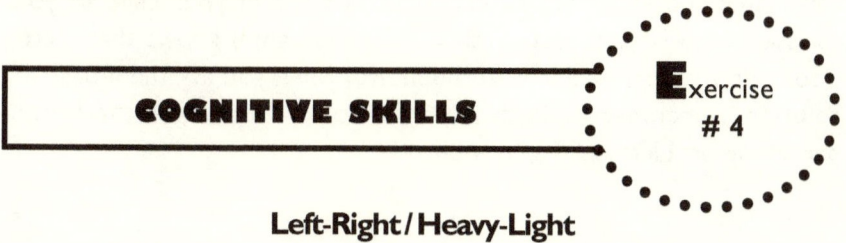

Exercise # 4

Left-Right / Heavy-Light

[Age 3-4] This **E**xercise helps teach your child the difference between left vs. right, and heavy vs. light. Collect objects from around the house or outdoors, then place the heavy objects (i.e. rock, book, and grapefruit, etc.) in one pile and the light objects (i.e. leaf, pencil, rag, etc.) in another pile. Now, ask your child to pick an heavy object up from the heavy pile with their right hand and a light object up fromt the light pile with their left hand. Then, ask them to tell you which is the heavier of the two items, and which hand it's located in.

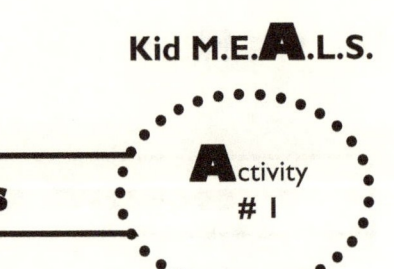

COGNITIVE SKILLS

Mental Rest & Physical Exercise

[Age: 3+] Being well rested and physically fit will effect your child's ability to digest and comprehend much of the information they take in during the course of a day. If your child is tired because they don't get the proper amount of sleep or excercise, they'll be less likely to use their mind to its full potential.

It all starts with a good night's rest. Early-age children require at least ten hours of sleep. Establish good sleeping habits early on, so your child becomes conditioned to getting to sleep at a reasonable hour.

Physical energy translates itself into mental energy. There are plenty of physical **A**ctivities that your child can engage in to to help them develop good fitness habits. Whether it's stretching, playing, dancing, or just jumping around and having fun, keeping your children active will keep them alert. But don't just convey the value of these habits of rest and exercise by enforcing them, make sure you set a good example for your child. When they notice you incorporating these principles into your life, they will be more inclined to develop similar habits in their own. Stay physically fit. Establish an exercise routine: join a health club; get involved in neighborhood sports; run; stretch; just do it! Not only will it keep you fit, energized, rested, and physical activity in your own life, it also demonstrates to your child a healthy lifestyle for them to subscribe to, as well.

Kid M.E.A.L.S.

COGNITIVE SKILLS — Activity # 2

Driving Knowledge

[Age: 4+] Make good use of the time you spend with your child while driving. "Driving time" offers you and your child a great opportunity to spend quality one-on-one time with them. Don't waist it! Take advantage of this time by verbally interacting with them. When you're not talking about what happened at preschool or their favorite backyard game, take some time to focus on building their aptitude with all sorts of academic games. Here are a few ideas:

1. **Math in Motion**—Math helps your child conceptualize the world from a very logical point of view. It's a good idea to get your child comfortable with the subject of math by making it easy and fun. While you're in the car together, have fun with numbers by asking your child simple math questions that can gradually become more difficult as they progress.
2. **Grammar on the Go**—Verbalize age-appropriate words to your child. Ask them to use them in a sentence. If they are very young, engage in "letter" games. Sing the alphabet or see if they can name the letter that comes after the one you pick. Or, ask them to read out letters or words on road signs.
3. **Mind Mixer**—Make up a story, and have your child tag on to the story with their own ideas of how it will play out. As the story moves back and forth taking on diifferent shape, it will force your kids to pay attention with each twist and turn.

COGNITIVE SKILLS

Activity #3

Smart Sense

[Age: 5+] Enhance your child's perception and awareness of touch, taste, smell, and sound through the following **A**ctivity. Sit with your child at the kitchen table. Blindfold them. Then, place the following items on the table in front of them: apple, cinnamon, and a teaspoon. Now, instruct them to use their senses to determine what the objects are. Using their sense of touch, start with the apple. Then, place the cinnamon under their nose asking them to use their sense of smell. Lastly, tap a spoon up against a bowl, and ask them to name the two items they hear. Once they've successfully completed the task, cut the apple into little pieces, place them in the bowl, add the cinnamon, top with some whipped cream as a bonus to recognize their accomplishment, and serve them the delicious treat.

Kid M.E.A.L.S.

COGNITIVE SKILLS — Activity # 4

Shape Hunt

[Age 3-4] Go on a street-sign hunt with your child, and locate different shapes. You can do this Activity while driving in your car with them. Point out all the different street signs, and see if your child can identify the shape of each one. Look for rectangular street signs, circular "do not enter" signs, square "school bus" signs, rectangular "yield" signs, square "speed limit" signs, etc. Ask your child questions along the way that encourage thinking and language skills, such as naming the letters in the signs or the words posted on it. Discuss their meaning, as well.

Kid M.E.A.L.S.

COGNITIVE SKILLS — Lesson

Wisdom in the Woods

[Age 5+] Make the science of nature fun to learn while playing in the woods. You can have fun learning about the nature and the environment and enjoy a day outdoors with them at the same time. There are plenty of ways you can incorporate educational Lessons into your day together. Here are a few science projects you and your child can conduct while playing outdoors.

1. **Park Pictures**—Take your camera to the park, especially one for your child. You'll have a great time recording all the outdoor nature sights. Once the pictures are developed, bring them home and frame them with creative captions next to each. Add the date and place a picture of you and your child in the middle that will remind you of your day together. Hang it up in their bedroom when it's completed.
2. **Something to Grow On**—This project requires you to read up on the different types of plants and trees that grow in the wild. Bring the book along to use it as a guide during your walk in the woods. You are sure to find plenty to compare and learn about. Identify some of the different forms of plant life and collect them in a bag. Bring them home to mat them in a frame. Label what you find in your collection and date your project. It can be hung up next to their "Park Pictures" collage.

Kid M.E.A.L.S.

COGNITIVE SKILLS — **S**tory

Smart to the Heart

[Age 4-5] Willie the Worm loved to play tic-tac-toe. So much, in fact, that he became the best player in the neighborhood. He played all the time with his friends, Rachael the Rabbit, Rocky the Raccoon, and Sammy the Squirrel. They would always try to beat him, but his love of the game made him unbeatable.

Then one day, he heard about a tic-tac-toe contest that was being held in the neighborhood. Excited about the tournament, Willie quickly wiggled his way back home to ask his mom if he could enter the contest. His mom said yes, but only if Willie agreed to follow one of her golden rules. She taught him from a very early age that *doing your best, being a good sport, and enjoying yourself, even if you lose, was much more important than winning—That's because you always learn something whether you win or lose.* When it was clear that Willie understood what his mom told him, she looked him the eye and gave him her wink of approval.

He and his friends practiced all week long. Willie won most of the time, but whenever he lost, it made him feel sad. But thinking about his mom's golden rule would cheer him up: *play your best, be a good sport, and enjoy yourself, even if you lose—that's because you always learn something whether you win or lose.* It made Willie feel a little better when he realized that his mom was right. Even though he felt lousy when he lost, he always learned what not to do the next time.

When he and his neighborhood friends arrived at the tournament the next day, Willie was ready to play. He did so well that he made it to the final match, and so did Rachael. They were the last two remaining contestants. Willie got so caught up in the contest that all he could think about was winning the tournament. As everyone watched on to see who would win, he looked into the crowd and noticed his mother looking on.

The contest led to a final match between Willie and his friend Rachael. Not before long, there were only a few more moves to be made before the contest would end. It was clear that Willie was about to beat Rachael. Willie waited all week for this moment, and he knew that Rachael had, too. Before he made his next move, his mother caught his eye and winked at him, just as she had done the day she reminded him about the golden rule. Suddenly, winning became less important to himself than knowing how bad his friend, Rachael, would feel if she had lost. Deep down inside himself he knew how smart he was, and that he could win if he really wanted to. Knowing he did his best, and learning something along the way, became more important than needing to show everyone how great a player he was. That's when he decided to place his X in a box which enabled Rachael to win the tournament.

Willie's mom knew he chose to let Rachael win, even though he could have. She hugged her son after the contest and winked at him, then said, "You really are smart, Willie, smart to the heart."

◆ Chapter 4 ◆

"You're only trying to migrate from yourself."

© The New Yorker Collection 2002, Bruce Eric Kaplan
Cartoonbank.com, All Rights Reserved

HONESTY

Hon•es•ty, n.—integrity; truthfulness; the quality or condition of being honest.

Being entirely honest with oneself is a good exercise.

—Sigmund Freud

Early on in life, a child's behavior will, for better or worse, mirror their parent's on many levels. Therefore, it's important to be a good role model first, then a good teacher, especially if you expect your child to become an honest person. Don't just tell them what to do—practice what you preach.

For many of us, our motivation for being honest stems from fears that our parents instilled within us during our early age years. However, if parents take the time to help their child recognize the value of being honest, then they will develop a *desire* to behave that way, not out of fear, but because they *want* to. Establishing this foundation will encourage them to cultivate a deeper and more authentic form of integrity as they grow up.

Parents, who use their power to help their child recognize the value of being honest, make it possible for them to develop this essential quality. The following "HONESTY" Kid M.E.A.L.S. are designed to support parents in their efforts to achieve this goal. It's never too early to begin nourishing the value of your child's integrity.

Kid M.E.A.L.S.

HONESTY — Message #1

[Age 4-6]   WORD of the Day

Honesty

Kid M.E.A.L.S.

HONESTY   Message #2

[Age 4-5]   QUIZ of the Day

Who is being honest in the three examples below?

(Circle your answer below the question)

Shane's father came home one evening and asked him who had broken the garage window. Even though Shane was sad because he broke the window after hitting it with a baseball, he admitted to his father that he was the one who broke it.

Shane was: **Honest**   or,   **Not Honest**

When little Rebecca went to the store yesterday with her mom she found someone's Barbie doll in the middle of the parking lot. As much as she would like to have kept it for herself, because she loves Barbie dolls so much, she showed her mom what she found. They brought it into the store and gave it to the manager because who ever owned it might come back to look for it.

Rebecca was: **Honest**   or,   **Not Honest**

Randy's mother asked him who knocked the trash can over in the basement without letting anyone know, but he was afraid to tell the truth so he told her that his younger sister had done it.

Randy was: **Honest**   or,   **Not Honest**

Kid M.E.A.L.S.

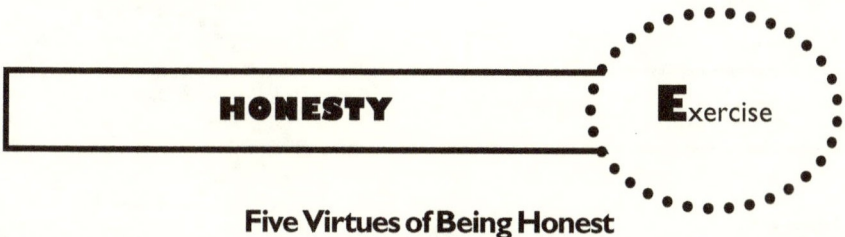

HONESTY — **E**xercise

Five Virtues of Being Honest

[Age 6+] This **E**xercise illustrates for your child the virtues of being honest. Through role playing you can help your children understand the importance of being honest. The objective of this **E**xercise is to demonstrate Five Virtues of Being Honest to your child: (1) it requires courage to accept responsibility for one's mistakes; (2) a person will be forgiven for being honest if their apology is sincere; (3) a person will get into more trouble by lying than by telling the truth; (4) apologizing makes people feel better; and, (5) telling the truth makes others trust you.

Start the role-playing by showing your child how to have the courage to be honest. Pretend that you accidentally stepped on one of their toys earlier that day and broke it. Have your child ask you if you know who broke the toy, then walk them through the following steps: (1) inform them that you have the courage to tell them the truth and that it was you who broke their toy; (2) ask your child with sincerity if they will forgive you for having the courage to be honest; (3) explain that you would be creating more problems for everyone if you lied and caused someone else to take the blame for what you had done; (4) apologize to your child and explain that you prefer to tell the truth because keeping lies inside of you makes you feel bad, and admitting them makes you feel better; and finally, (5) explain that you want to tell the truth because a person's trust means a lot to you. Now reverse the roles and have your child respond accordingly.

HONESTY

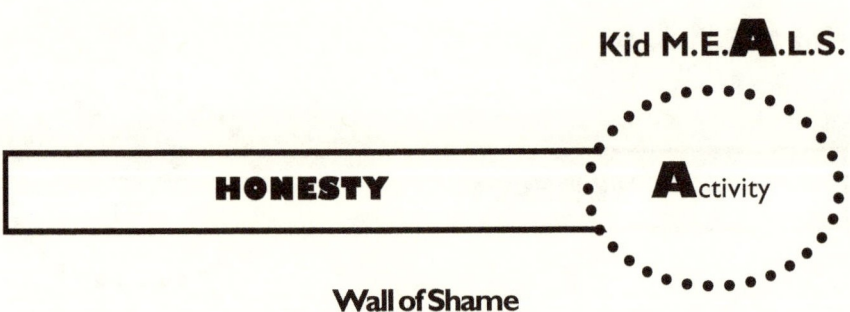

Wall of Shame

[Age 5+] People will lie to avoid embarrassment or punishment for having done something wrong. When they try to cover up the lie, things get very complicated because they have to remember what they said and what they did not say. Think about how much energy it takes to cover a lie compared to having the courage to tell the truth. In the long run, it's easier to tell the truth and we become free from the worry of hiding the lie.

For this **A**ctivity you will need to clip out stories in the newspaper that revolve around people who were shamed because they got caught lying, cheating, or stealing. Perhaps, a popular sports figure got into trouble and as a result, he got kicked out of the league. Not only did he let his teammates down, he also shamed himself, his family, and his friends. Clip these types of stories out of the paper and tack them up to a wall labeled "Wall of Shame."

Kid M.E.A.L.S.

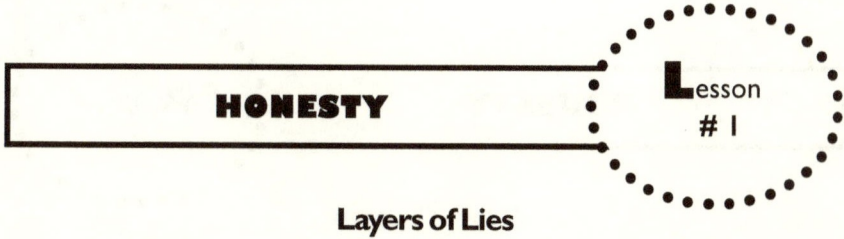

Layers of Lies

[Age 5+] This Lesson illustrates that when a person lies they separate themselves from their true self. It requires seven paper cups and a marker. On one cup write your child's name with the word *truth* beneath it. On the others write the word *lie*. Now, explain to your child that each time they lie they are covering themselves up with layers of lies that hide them, not only from the truth, but from themselves, as well. To exemplify this concept place a cup labeled *lie* over the cup with your child's name on it and insert another *lie* cup inside the cup with their name. Ask them if the word truth is being covered up by the cup labeled, lie, while you are doing this. When they respond yes, explain that each time you tell a lie you cover up the truth a little bit more until the lies build up around you so much (continue placing the remainder of the cups inside and outside the cup labeled with your child's name on it) that eventually it becomes difficult to find the truth.

Now fill the cup with water and extend the analogy further by comparing the weight of the water to the weight of the lies you must live with when you fill your life with them. Go to the sink and explain that, "It's best not to tell lies so you can avoid the weight that lying builds up inside you." Dump the water out of the cup and pull all the cups from the bottom one with the word, *truth,* printed on it. Hold the *truth* cup up and finish the Lesson by saying, "As many layers of lies that can pile up on top of the truth, deep down, it's always going to be there."

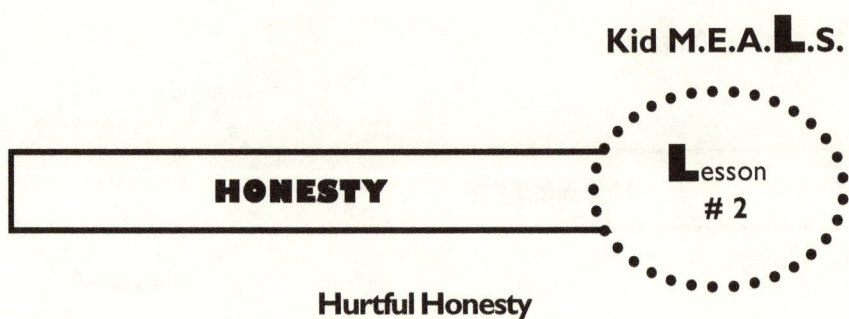

HONESTY

Hurtful Honesty

[Age 5+] Honesty is telling the truth. However, it's important for a child to learn that there are times when the truth can hurt someone's feelings. Here's a simple way to teach them this valuable Lesson to help discourage such behavior. Ask them the following questions.

> **Question:** If someone asks you about something that you do not wish to share, what can you say that is honest, and at the same time won't hurt their feelings?
>
> **Answer:** I'd rather not share that right now, I hope you understand.

There are also circumstances when people can be cruel even though they are telling the truth.

> **Question:** When is being too honest not really honesty, but a lack of respect or meanness toward another person?
>
> **Answer:** When it hurts the feelings of others.

Kid M.E.A.L.S.

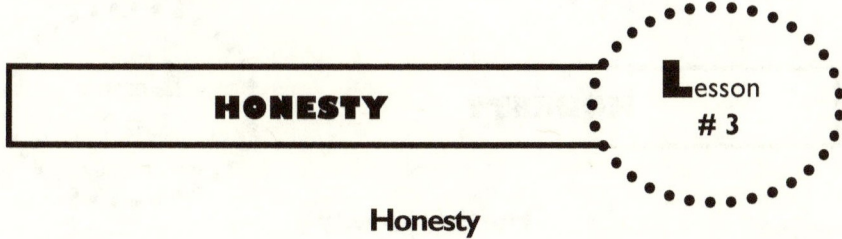

Honesty

[Age 5+] This discussion Lesson touches on the topic of why people sometimes do not tell the truth.

1. **Why do you think people do <u>not</u> tell the truth sometimes?**

   Their response: (Give them an opportunity to answer you)

   Your response: Often it is because they don't want to get in trouble or because they don't want someone to get mad at them or be disappointed in them. We all want people to like us. So, sometimes we try to hide things so we don't get in trouble and so they don't get mad or disappointed.

2. **What happens when people find out we lied?**

   Their response: (Give them an opportunity to answer you)

   Your response: They get even madder and more disappointed, and we get ourselves further into trouble. And if we lie once, they may not trust we are telling the truth later on.

3. **Do we want people to trust us?**

   Their response: (Give them an opportunity to answer you)

   Your response: It's important for people to trust us. When there's lots of trust between people, they feel safe and loved. But, it sometimes takes courage to tell the truth. For instance, when something goes wrong, or when we did something we weren't supposed to do, you need to be brave enough to tell the truth.

HONESTY

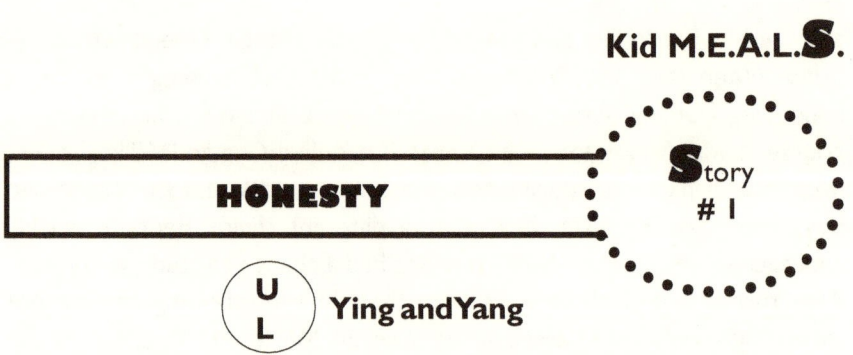

Story #1

(U / L) **Ying and Yang**

[Age 4-6] When kids make decisions about right and wrong, how do they know which is the best direction for them to take? The forces of right and wrong pull us all in opposite directions. However, when we listen to ourselves deep down we instinctively know the difference between right and wrong. Even though we find ourselves wishing from time to time that we made better choices, what's important is that we use what we learned in order to avoid making future mistakes. This enables a person to be more responsible as they take into consideration how their choices can impact the outcome of their behavior. Building an emotional and mental bridge that gets your child to think about outcomes will help you accomplish this goal. Encourage your child to value the decisions they make by sharing the following **S**tory with them.

One day, Willie the Worm was in Shane's (substitute with your child's name) backyard playing with his neighbors, Ying and Yang—the twin turtles. It was the first hot day of spring. The boys just got home from school and talked about going down to take a dip in the pond. Yang said to Willie and his brother Ying, "I've got a great idea, since it's so hot out this afternoon let's put our bathing suits on and go down to the pond!" "That's a great idea," said Willie. Let's put on our swim trunks and meet back here in five minutes." Just as they were about to run off, Ying yelled, "Wait a minute, we can't go, I just remembered that we all have to take our last 'spelling' exam of the school year. If any of us fails the test, we'll have to go to summer school to make up for it. If that happens, no one will be going swimming." "Ah, phooey," replied, Yang. "The test is tomorrow; we'll worry about it later. Now let's go, time is running out." Ying just didn't feel right about going. As much as he would have like to have gone down to the pond that hot afternoon, he knew deep down that the right thing to do was stay home and study for his big test the next day. He realized that he needed to put off the swimming for another time in order to avoid failing such an important test. So he *decided* to stay home and study, while Willie and Yang *chose* to spend their time down at the pond. When Yang and Willie returned home that evening, they didn't make Ying feel any better by telling him about all the fun he missed. Of course, it wasn't easy for Ying to hear. But, unlike Yang and Willie, he was prepared to pass the spelling test the following day, and the other two boys were not, because they made a different *choice*. Bedtime quickly approached, and neither Willie nor Yang had a chance to study very much. As it turned out all three boys took the test the following day, but not surprisingly, only Ying passed it. As a result, Willie and Yang wound up spending most of their summer days in school, while Ying spent most of his down at the pond.

Up-Link
MOTTO of the Day

Choose to do the right thing!

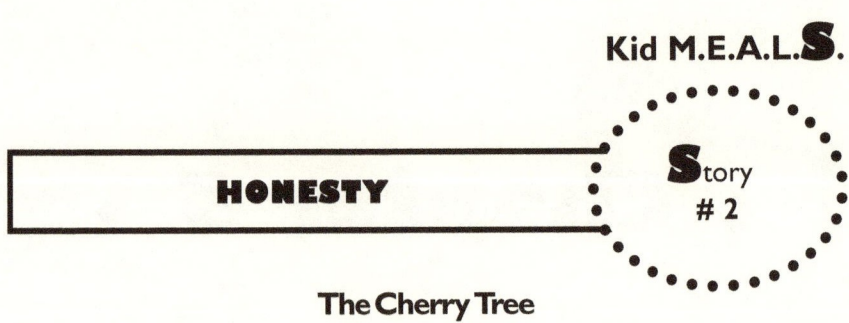

The Cherry Tree

[Age 4-6] This **S**tory is an age-old classic that represents the value of being honest. A six-year-old boy named George Washington was tossing his father's hatchet into a beautiful cherry tree that sat on their front lawn. Without realizing it, little George dug the axe into the old cherry tree so many times that it caused the tree to die. When his father discovered his favorite tree dying he took a closer look and noticed that someone had damaged the trunk with deep hatchet marks. He came into the house with great anger and demanded to know who had killed his cherry tree. Just then, his son George came into the room holding his hatchet. "George," said his father with rage in his voice, "do you know who has killed the cherry tree?" This was a difficult question for little George to answer, because he knew that he was the one who had damaged the tree with his axe and he was upset that he'd let his father down. As he stood there in front of his father frozen with fear, his father demanded to know who was responsible for killing the tree. Fearful, yet brave, little George managed to find the courage to tell his father the truth. Bracing himself for the consequences little George cried out, "I cannot tell a lie, Father. I cut the cherry tree with my hatchet." In reaction to his son's bravery and honesty, the anger in his father's face was swept away. With his mother proudly standing off to the side, his father looked him in the eyes and said, "My son, that you should not be afraid to tell the truth is worth more than a thousand cherry trees with gold leaves!"

♦ Chapter 5 ♦

"We're encouraging people to become involved in their own rescue."

SELF-RELIANCE

re•li•ance, *n.*—dependence upon one's self; confidence, in one's self; self-sufficient.

If it is to be, it is up to me.

—*William H. Johnsen*

Self-reliance, like your child's other attributes, becomes a stronger part of their character when parents demonstrate its value to them at an early age. Small doses can begin to condition them so they have some understanding of what it means to be self-sufficient later in life.

Be careful not to do everything for your child. Parents who do so deny them the opportunity to become self-reliant. Understandably, there are a lot of things that children simply cannot do for themselves. However, if it's because you are too busy to take time out of your hectic schedule to teach them how to be self-reliant, then how can you expect them to learn how to become that way. Parents who do everything for their child send them a message that it's okay not be self-reliant, because someone else will figure out how to do things for you. Unfortunately, once it's time to enter the real world it becomes very difficult for them to behave in a self-sufficient manner.

Individuals who do not become self-sufficient end up placing their welfare in other people hands. They build outside sources of support in order to get what they need. Thus they become beholden upon others to get things done. Being self-reliant does not mean that you are opposed to support from outside sources. It means that you accept help when you need it, but don't expect others to do the things you can just because you're unwilling to do them for yourself.

"SELF-RELIANCE" Kid M.E.A.L.S. are designed to help parents develop self-sufficient forms of behavior within their early age child. When parents use their power in creative ways to encourage the formation of this type of behavior, it enhances their child's chances of being responsible later in life.

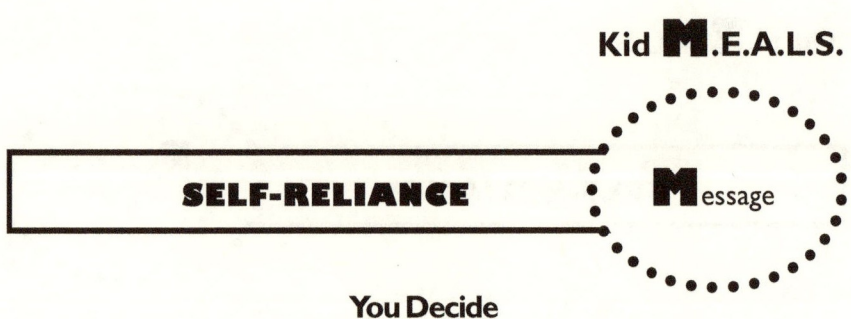

SELF-RELIANCE

You Decide

[Age 3-5] Parents who foster their child's ability to make decisions on their own help them develop self-reliance. Send them a **M**essage throughout the day that inspires their decision-making skills. It should begin when they wake up in the morning by letting them decide which color shirt to wear. At lunchtime, ask them what they would like to eat and give them several *choices*. Or, if you find them whining about something, it's a great opportunity to present *choices* that reveal alternative ways for them to control the situation in order to relieve their frustration. For instance, if they try to delay going to bed, tell them they have a *choice*: they can get into their pajamas and have enough time to hear you read them a story, or continue doing what they were doing, but when the time comes for them to go to bed; they must live with their *choice*. Being firm about when bedtime comes is important if parents expect their child to accept the consequences for the decisions they choose to make.

By giving your child an age-appropriate opportunity to make choices, you are sending them the **M**essage that you respect their capability to make them. Furthermore, children who feel empowered to become decision makers are more likely to move through obstacles, feel in control of their lives, and become self-reliant.

Kid M.E.A.L.S.

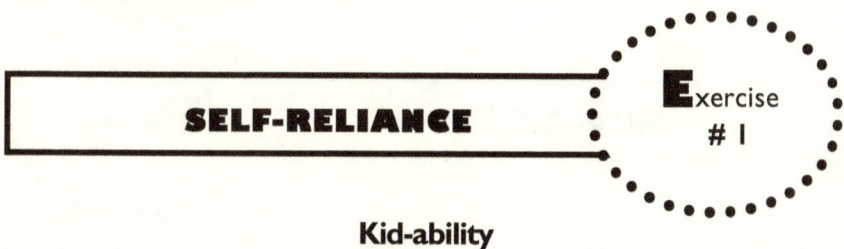

SELF-RELIANCE — Exercise #1

Kid-ability

[Age 5+] Perform the following Exercise one evening after you get home from work. Let your children know that you are going to give them an opportunity to take charge and become the decision maker in the household. Inform them that they are responsible for making the decisions and resolve any problems that might come up throughout the course of the night. If they are graded well at the end of the evening, reward them with a weekend family barbeque. In order to pass the test, they'll need to do everything for themselves: taking charge of the games or activities that the family might engage in, cleaning up any projects that they may begin, finding things they may have misplaced, getting snacks on their own, getting ready for bed, picking up after themselves, washing up and brushing their teeth, and turning off all the lights before they go to bed. When you put them down for the evening, spend time talking about how they felt being in charge. Did they like it? Was it more difficult than they expected, and why?

Instilling your child with a sense of responsibility doesn't mean that they are going to be running the household any time soon. However, it will lay the groundwork for what will eventually be a part of their everyday life.

SELF-RELIANCE

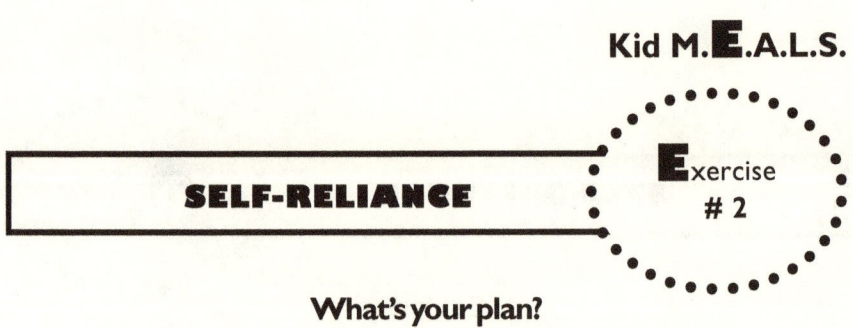

Kid M.**E**.A.L.S.

Exercise # 2

What's your plan?

[Age 5+] Before you're about to do something with your children announce, "I've got a plan!" Even when you're about to do something that doesn't include them, make the same declaration. Eventually, your child will mimic you and begin saying, "I've got a plan!" prior to taking on a particular task. When you hear your child use the phrase, draw attention to it and acknowledge the fact that they've used it by asking, "What did you say your plan is? That's a great plan!"

Up-Link
QUESTION of the Day

What's your plan?

Kid M.E.A.L.S.

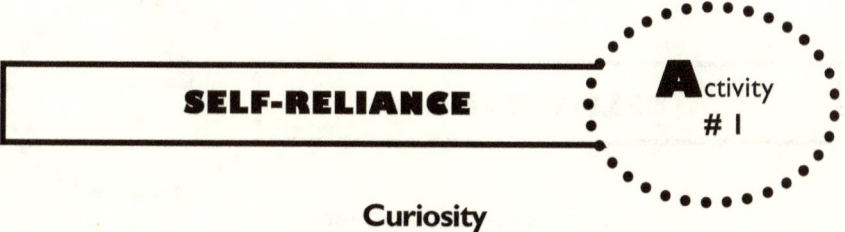

SELF-RELIANCE

Curiosity

[Age 5+] This self-reliance-building Activity takes advantage of your child's natural curiosity. The next time they ask you a question instead of just answering them off the top of your head, help them become more resourceful by introducing them to a dictionary, online information and education sources, library, or books and magazines on the subject. This way, they'll learn where to find answers to their questions, and also that there are multiple sources of information they can rely on. The key is to make the Activity simple, even fun, so they instinctively think about it the next time their curiosity surfaces.

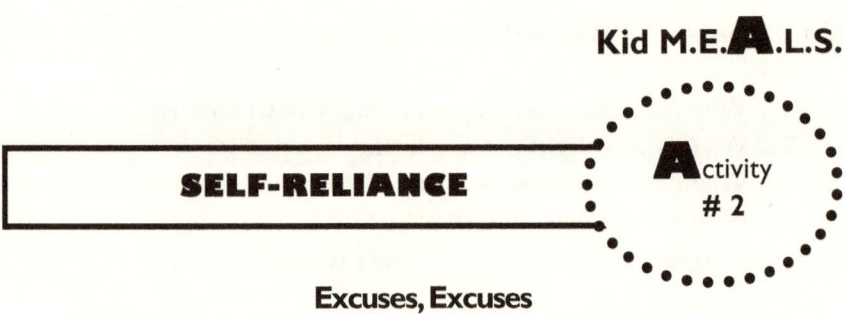

SELF-RELIANCE

Excuses, Excuses

[Age 5+] Making your child understand the difference between excuses and accountability helps him avoid the natural tendency we all have, which is to blame others for things that we do not want to admit we are responsible for. The following **A**ctivity encourages your child to take responsibility for his or her own actions. At least two children and you are needed to play. Label five index cards with the word *excuse* on them, five with the words *good reason* on them, and five with the word *question* on them.

On the five "excuse" cards, write the following five excuses—one per card—on each:

1. You never told me to do it.
2. My sister told me to do it.
3. I'm not hungry.
4. I was just playing.
5. He didn't ask me to give it back to him.

On the five "good reason" cards write the following five good reasons—one per card—on each:

1. You didn't need to tell me, I knew better.
2. Even though my sister told me to do it, I shouldn't have.
3. I'm not hungry, because I ate a snack before dinner.
4. I was running through the living room, when the vase broke.
5. I should have just given it back to him, because it's his.

On the "question" cards write the following questions:

1. Why didn't you clean up your room this morning?
2. Why did you let the dog outside?
3. Why do you need to eat your dinner?
4. How did the vase break?
5. Why didn't you give your friend's toy back to him?

Combine the "excuse" and "good reason" decks and shuffle them together. Stack them; face down, so the "excuse" and "good reason" labels are hidden. Place the pile of "questions," facing down, next to the other pile.

Begin the game by taking a card off the top of the "questions" deck, and reading one of the questions. Your child will then remove a card from the "excuse" / "good reason" stack—read the question out load. After they hear it, they must determine whether or not the statement is an excuse or good reason. They receive a point for every correct answer. The person with the most points after reading all the cards in the "outcome" deck wins!

SELF-RELIANCE

Kid M.E.A.**L**.S.

Lesson

Plan for Safety

[Age 5+] Children need to learn how to rely on themselves when it comes to emergency situations. The following **Lesson** in first aid helps them plan what to do in case of an emergency. It will be comforting to know that your child had a **Lesson** in safety before a mishap occurs. It also gives them a sense of security and confidence knowing they have some understanding of what to expect if such an event should occur. Review with your child a simple plan of safety that outlines what to do in the two following emergency situation:

1. **What to do if there's a fire**—conduct a fire drill; show them how to get out of the house, and teach them that dialing 911 is only to be done in emergency situations; also, make a list of emergency telephone numbers that you'll post near each telephone, etc.
2. **What to do if someone gets hurt**—pretend that someone gets hurt badly and act out what to do; encourage them to look for an adult; if an adult is not around, point out the emergency numbers near the telephone so they can dial to get help.

These two **Lessons** are just a great start to building your child's ability to be self-reliant.

Kid M.E.A.L.S.

SELF-RELIANCE

Attention Seeker

[Age 4-6] This Story illustrates what happens when a person "cries wolf" to get attention because they want everyone else to do things for them, instead of relying on themselves to get what they need.

One day, Willie the Worm heard someone howling at the top of a small hill. He crawled his way up to the top to see what all the commotion was about. When he got there, he realized it was his friend, Shelly the Sheepdog, howling over her flock of sheep. He asked her if everything was okay, and Shelly told him that she thought she just saw a wolf, so she began howling for help. "Since you're here," she asked, "Could you do me a big favor—could you go back down the hill to fetch me a drink of water?" Willie was more than happy to do his friend a favor. After doing so, he made his way back down the hill, and when he got to the bottom heard Shelly crying, wolf, once again. Shelly must have seen another wolf, he thought to himself... So, like a good friend he crawled back up the hill to see if everything was okay. But, it was another false alarm—there were no wolves in sight.

Exhausted from his climb, Willie asked, "What is it now, Shelly?" "Ah, nothing," I just thought I saw another wolf about to attack my flock... It must have been my imagination," she replied. Then, she asked Willie if he wouldn't mind, since he was there already, going back down to get her another drink of water. She'd been out in the sun all morning, and she was still so very thirsty. Being the friendly type that he was, Willie agreed to help her out again. So, he headed back down the hill and came back with Shelly's water. "Enjoy the rest of the day," he said as he headed back down the hill. But Before Willie got down to the bottom of the hill, he heard the loud, piercing, familiar cry coming from the top of the hill again, and he thought to himself—I wonder if Shelly is whining because she sees a wolf or she is just doing it to get my attention so she can get another drink of water? He wasn't interested in making another trip back up the hill just so he could get her another glass of water, but he was concerned about her because this time she might have been in trouble. In response to her yelling, he quickly scooted back up the hill, only to find Shelly waiting there to ask him for another glass of water. This time Willie complained to her, saying, "Shelly, you keep crying wolf, and every time I get here, there's no wolf! I think you're just trying to get my attention, so you can get me to go down the hill to get you a glass of water because you don't want to do it yourself? You need to stop crying wolf! If you want a glass of water, just go down to the bottom of the hill yourself instead of making someone else do it for you." But she ignored Willie's plea. Shelly looked at him when he was done speaking, as though she hadn't heard a word he said, and asked, "Willie, since you're already up here, could you fetch me just one more glass of water?" "Oh boy, not again," Willie muttered. "You're going to have to get your own glass of water Shelly; I've got to get back home for lunch." As he made his way down the hill, he heard Shelly's howling cries once again. Willie didn't wonder any longer about what she really needed. He knew that she just wanted was to ask someone to get her a glass of water, because she was too lazy to do it herself. Getting others to do things for you might work for a while, he thought to himself, but if you always "cry wolf" eventually everyone is going to stop listening to you.

♦ Chapter 6 ♦

"On the other hand, it's not going to put any artificial limits on the power of a child's imagination."

© The New Yorker Collection 2003, Drew Dernavich
Cartoonbank.com, All Rights Reserved

CREATIVITY

cre•a•tive, *n.*—having the ability or power to create; characterized by originality and expressiveness; imagination.

Imagination is the highest kite one can fly.

—Lauren Bacall

Children are naturally curious and creative. All they require is the proper guidance early on so they will feel comfortable expressing their individuality and their creativity as they grow up. If they are not encouraged to discover their creative talent and energy, they may never learn to appreciate the freedom, beauty, and wonder that comes from being creative.

Children who believe their ideas are valuable are not afraid to express themselves. When they establish the confidence to view things from a different point-of-view, they develop the courage to express what's inside them. This also gives a child the freedom to act "differently" so they can be original, and have the confidence to try new things.

"CREATIVITY" Kid M.E.A.L.S. are designed to nourish this quality within your early-age child. The primary objective behind serving them is to supply your child's imagination with interesting ideas that will begin to build their creative confidence and awareness.

Kid M.E.A.L.S.

CREATIVITY — Message #1

[Age 4] WORD of the Day

Imagination

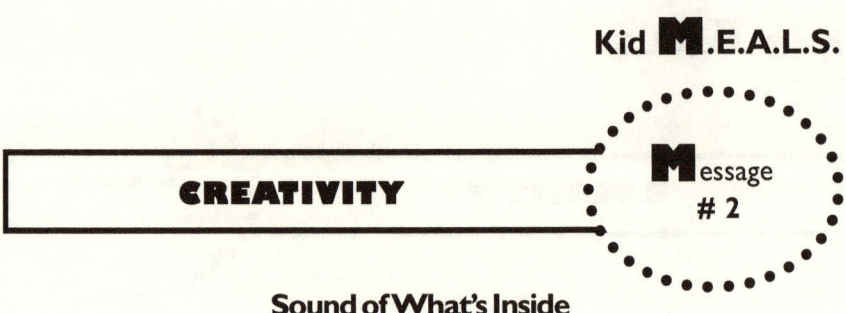

CREATIVITY

Sound of What's Inside

[Age 3-4] Leave behind a simple musical instrument one morning on the breakfast table, such as a harmonica or bongo drum, with the following Message of inspiration:

Make some noise with musical toys

—

Don't ever hide what's deep inside

Kid M.E.A.L.S.

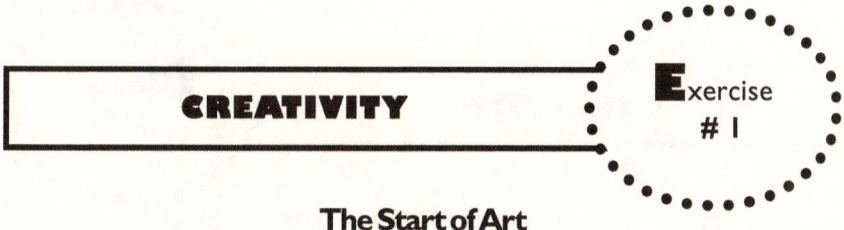

CREATIVITY

The Start of Art

[Age 3-5] Many people grow up believing that art is only for fancy people, while it is in fact something all of us can appreciate. Introduce art, perhaps a printed copy or even something ripped out of a magazine, to your child, so their mind can begin exploring artistic design at a young age. Here's an **E**xercise that encourages them to begin experiencing art in a challenging, yet fun way.

Day 1: Leave behind a simple sketch for your child and challenge them to search through the picture to look for particular colors, shapes, or objects of your choosing.

Day 2: Leave behind a copy of a more sophisticated work of art, such a Monet's famous *Water Lilies*, and ask them to search through that picture to look for particular colors and shapes, just as they did the prior day.

When you come home from work later that evening, have fun discussing how successful they were identifying all the shapes and colors you challenged them to find in the pictures you left behind. Ask them what they liked most about the picture. This is a great way to make art a fun and interesting part of their life.

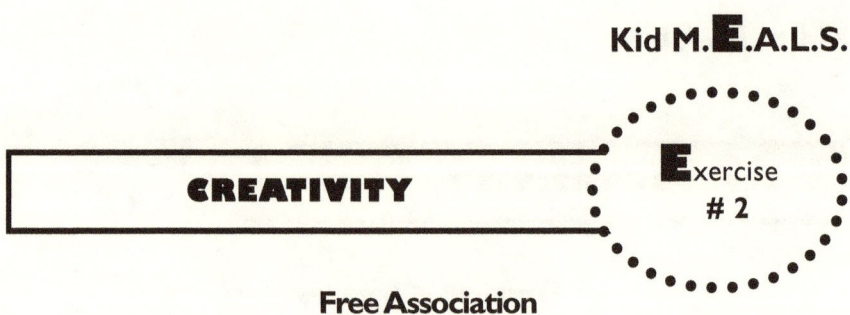

CREATIVITY

Free Association

[Age 4-6] Stretch your child's imagination by turning a fun game of free association into an Exercise that you can engage in while driving in your automobile. Announce a word that they can relate to such as *playground*, and ask them to blurt out what they think of immediately. Not only will this game help expand your child's imagination; it enables you to become more aware of how they see the world.

Here is a list of words that you can begin with:

Breakfast	Scary	Happy
School	Funny	Sad
Games	Beach	Sports
Music	Friend	Family

Kid M.E.A.L.S.

CREATIVITY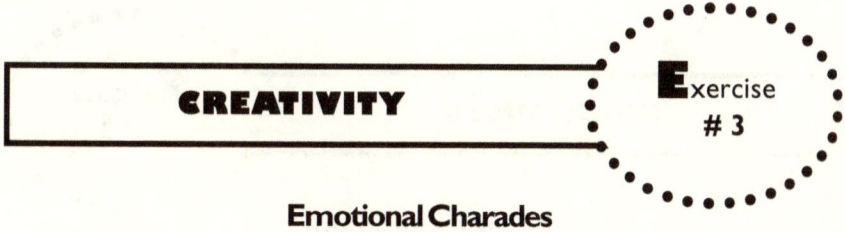

Emotional Charades

[Age 4-6] Restricting your child's ability to communicate without the aid of verbal language will force them to develop their creative talents. A great **E**xercise game to help develop your child's imagination and get them in touch with emotional forms of expression can be achieved through the ever-popular game, "charades." Players get one minute to communicate an emotion by creatively miming (physical gestures) them to their teammate. Whoever identifies the most number of emotion words, wins. Here are few simple words to start out with:

Happy
Straight eyebrows, closed mouth bent upward.

Sad
Lowered eyebrows, closed mouth bent downward.

Fear
Lowered eyebrows, moderately open mouth with upper lip bent downward.

Anger
Raised eyebrows, moderately open mouth with upper lip curved downward.

Surprised
Highly raised eyebrows, very open mouth.

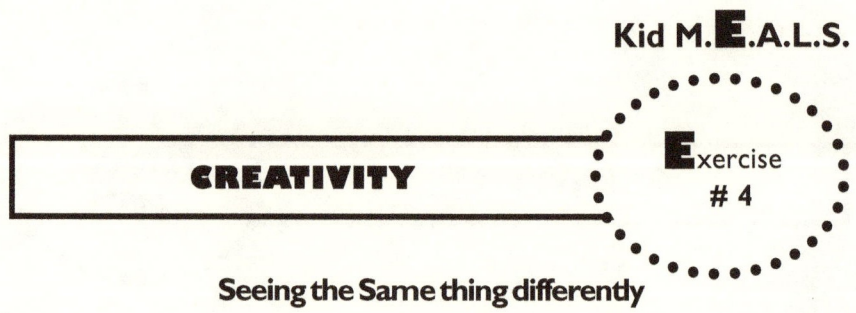

CREATIVITY

Seeing the Same thing differently

[Age 5-6] Being creative requires an open mind. This **Exercise** encourages your child to look at the same thing differently.

Draw a circle and a square on the front and back of separate pieces of paper. Starting with the circle, ask your child to look at it and tell you what they see. After they respond correctly, by saying a circle, turn the page to the backside, and this time, ask them to use their imagination to think about what else the circle could represent, for instance, a wheel. See how many they can be creative enough to think of. Here are a few that the circle can represent:

    Ball   Nickel   Moon   Pizza   Hole

Write down their response beneath the circle shape. Then, do the same **Exercise** using the square shape. Here are a few examples of what the square shape can represent:

    Box   Television   Ice   Cube   Pillow

Likewise, write the different ideas about the shape beneath the square drawing.

After you and your child are done having fun naming the different shapes, turn the two pages over and remind them that the only thing they saw at the beginning of the **Exercise** was a simple circle and square. Because they were able to think of *different* images in their mind, they were able to see many other things.

Kid M.E.A.L.S.

CREATIVITY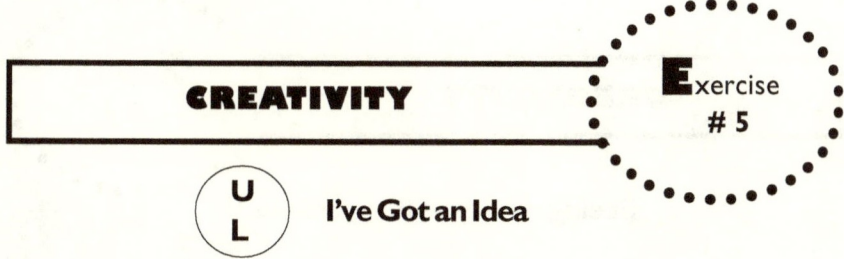

U L — I've Got an Idea

[Age 4-6] Children who come up with ideas on their own are creative and independent. The goal of this Exercise is to begin enhancing their creative confidence by planting the catch phrase, "I've got an idea" in their mind.

This Exercise needs to be carried out just before you engage your child in some type of activity or game. If, for example, you know that you're going to ask your child if they want to ride bikes around the neighborhood, instead of just asking, "Shane (substitute with your child's name), would you like to ride bikes now?"—say, with enthusiasm, "*I've got an idea*, (pause and wait until they acknowledge you] let's ride bikes." Here's another example, lets say you're both about to watch a video together, instead of asking, "Would you like to watch a movie?"—Say, "*I've got an idea,* (pause and wait until they acknowledge you) let's watch a movie!" Don't just ask them if they'd like to play checkers, precede the question with the catch phrase, "*I've got an idea*, lets play checkers!" Back the statement up with enthusiasm, so you draw their attention to the phrase.

If you're consistent, you will encourage your child to adopt the mentality

Up-Link
<u>MESSAGE of the Day</u>

I've got an idea!

CREATIVITY

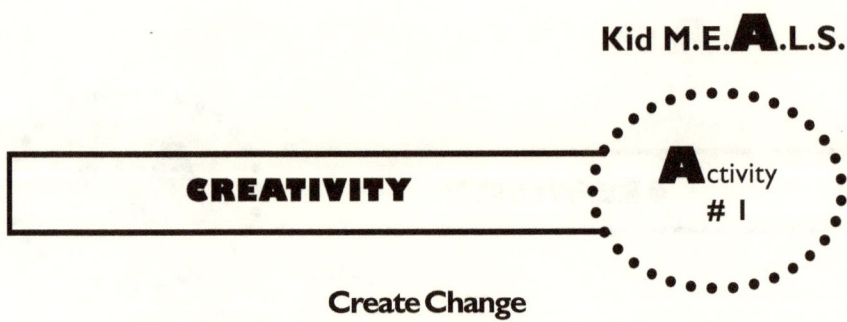

Kid M.E.A.L.S.

Activity #1

Create Change

[Age 3-4] Don't be shy about introducing your child to new experiences and new people. Be supportive and enthusiastic about taking new approaches to pre-established routines. When your child does things the same way over and over, or sees you doing the same thing repeatedly, they become comfortable and set in their ways. Try new things! Here are some ideas:

1. Go to different parks, playgrounds, and play centers on the weekends. Don't keep going back to the same places. Visit new places together.
2. Whether driving your kids to school or perhaps the soccer field, instead of taking the normal route there, try a new way. Point out that you're trying to get their from a different direction and interested in seeing new things along the way, too.
3. If they're interested in a particular sport, encourage them to try a new activity, like music lessons, karate, bowling, or swimming.
4. Invite new people over to your home for dinner. Encourage them to meet other people outside their neighborhood and family circle.

It may take a little more time and effort to think of new ways to approach established habits. However, if you are willing to go out of your way to try new things so will your child.

Kid M.E.A.L.S.

CREATIVITY — Activity # 2

Circus Act

[Age 4-6] Kids feel great about themselves when they physically perform in creative ways. Have fun pretending you and your child are performing a circus act together. Stage a show that the two of you create, direct, and videotape.

Begin this Activity by choreographing a series of simple acrobatic routines. Organize the show by outlining the act on individual index cards. Now, practice your routine. Then, perform for your audience. You may want to videotape your act while you're at it. Play fun music in the background. Here's a series of creative acts maneuvers to get you started.

- **Reverse Flip**—With your child standing face forward, have them bend over and place their hands between their legs. Now, bend down over them and grab their hands between their legs. Pull them up, and they'll flip upward.
- **High Wire Act**—Lay a piece of rope on the ground and let you child pretend they are walking on a high wire.
- **Stilt Walk**—Have your child stand on your feet, hold their hands to keep them balanced, and move around the room like they're walking on stilts.
- **The Grand Finale**—Kneel down on your left knee, hoist your child on your upright knee with their left foot, while holding on to their outstretched left hand. Together, bow to your audience.

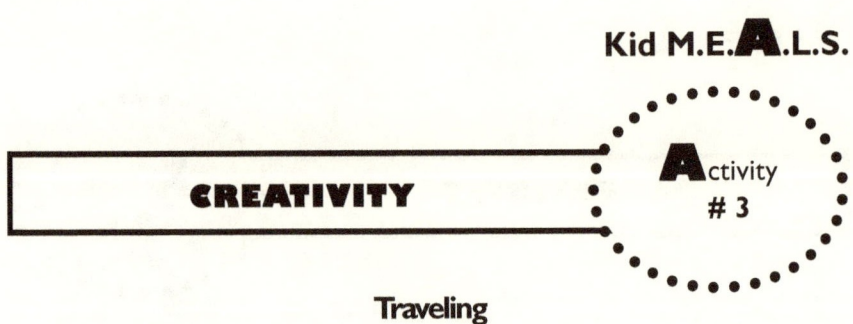

CREATIVITY

Traveling

[Age 4+] Traveling is a great way to expand your child's world and make it a more creative place. Meeting new people, discovering new places, and learning new customs, will broaden their point-of-view. It's also a lot of fun for everyone. Make it a habit of leaving behind the creature comforts of your own home and community, and broaden your child's horizons. A key ingredient to living creatively is by feeding your child's heart and mind with a fresh perspective that traveling to new places will offer them. Best of all, you can expose your child to new and interesting experiences without going very far or spending a lot of money.

If you live in the suburbs, a trip just into town can be an educational and eye-opening experience that will expand your child's view of the world. The converse applies to children who live in the city and travel to the country side. There are plenty of places you can go on a shoestring budget. Here are a few more suggestions:

- **Shore Points/Lakes**—lighthouses, fishing docks
- **Mountains**—canoeing, camping, cave towns
- **Historic Sites**—battlefields, memorials
- **Sports**—baseball or football game in another town or city

Make sure, when you do get away, that you spend time getting to know about the area, people, and their customs. These are the types of experiences which help expand your child's imagination about the world they live in.

Kid M.E.A.**L**.S.

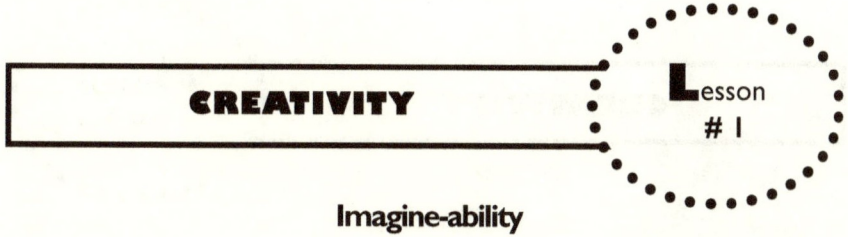

CREATIVITY

Lesson #1

Imagine-ability

[Age 3-4] Demonstrate for your child *how* to use their imagination. Teach them a **Lesson** that takes them through the steps to being creative. Kick start the process by spontaneously suggesting a fun scenario, such as the beach, where you can act out your make-believe game. Jump into your bathing suit and sandals. Come back into the room, and run your hand across the floor and say, "Let's build a sand castle, but not too close to the shoreline, or else a big wave might wash it away." Pull their imagination further into the picture by getting them involved in the design of your castle, then ask, "Do you want our castle to have one or two levels?" Allow them to answer, and then prompt them to use their imagination in all sorts of ways:

1. Determine what the size of the castle will be.
2. Plan to include tunnels.
3. Think about the number of sections.

If they haven't asked by now what you are going to build the sand castle with, point to building blocks, Legos, or anything that is around the house that can be used to build a make-believe sand castle. The more creative you are, the more you will be encouraging your child to act the same way. Have fun. Use all sorts of props to stretch their imagination: rulers can be used to simulate bridges; plastic cups become towers; towels can surround the castle to act as a moat; include their toy action figures to bring the castle to life; cut out paper flags and tape them to the cup towers—the more ways you can show them how to bring their creative energy to make-believe games like this one, the more apt they'll be to do it on their own.

Whether it's sand castles, adventure out at sea, or saving a princess from a fire-breathing dragon, demonstrating for your child how to tap into their creative energy will quickly turn a **Lesson** into habit.

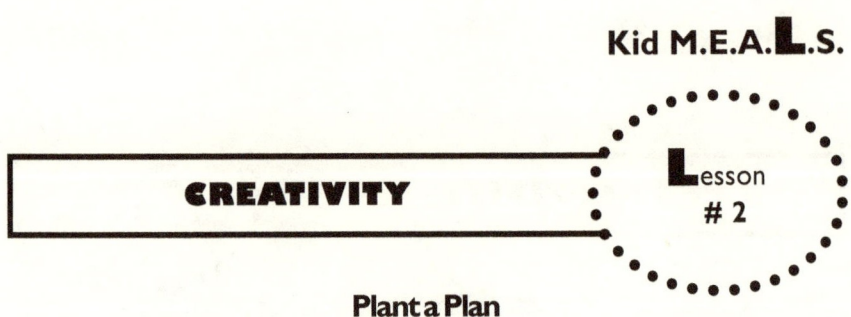

CREATIVITY

Plant a Plan

[Age 4+] Show your child how to make planning a part of the creative process. Create a garden with your child. Take out a piece of paper, and have them design the shape of *their* garden. Then, have them use their imagination outlining the type of plants and colors they'd like to see included in the design. Have them mark on the garden plan where they'd like the plants to go. Show them how to get creative by suggesting they add a birdbath that can be made out of a painted ceramic plate. Make certain that you steer the Lesson, so they feel in control of the process as much as possible. With the plan in their hand, and a list of supplies needed for the project, take them to a garden store and have fun picking out the plants and materials. Pick a spot in the yard, and following *their* plan. Be flexible, but stick to the original design as much as possible.

Once the garden has been created, step back with your child and compare the original plan to the finished product. This learning Lesson helps your child realize how they can bring their imagination to life. In addition, they see a connection between what they imagined it could look like—and what it looks like in actuality. It's also rewarding for them to watch their garden blossom during the weeks to come. In addition to nourishing their creative confidence, it will give them a sense of accomplishment that reinforces the value behind creative planning.

Kid M.E.A.L.S.

CREATIVITY

Story #1

Creative Problem Solving

[Age 3-5] Problem solving requires creativity. Here is a simple **S**tory that demonstrates how Willie the Worm and his friends came up with a creative solution to solve their problem. Solving problems will be a part of your child's daily routine throughout life. Instill your child with a sense of creativity that helps prevent them from getting frustrated because they are not sure what to do when confronted with problems. When you're creative, you can figure out ways to work around problems. Turn problem solving into a welcome challenge, instead of a burden.

Willie the Worm—No Problem

Willie the Worm was down by the creek one day with his friend Rachael the Rabbit when they ran into a buddy of theirs, Rocco the Raccoon, who lived on the other side of the creek. Rocco, was standing by the waterline, waving them over to the other side. Next to Rocco was a huge pile of walnuts and berries that he had just picked, and he wanted to share them with his friends. However, there was a problem for Willie and Rachael. The creek was so wide and deep that they were unable to cross over to the other side. It was a shame because Rachael loved walnuts and berries more than any other food, and right about now, she was feeling very hungry. Perhaps that's why she was so determined to find a way over to the other side. She scratched her head and waited a moment for a creative idea to come to her. She thought and thought and thought, until all of a sudden an idea popped into her head. "I got it," she said with a big smile on her face, "I know how we can solve this problem and get to the other side—we'll make a bridge!" "Are you sure that it will work, Rachael?" questioned Willie. "We won't know unless we try," she replied. Rachael pointed to a very tall tree that rose up higher than any other tree in the woods and said, "That's how we are going to get across, as soon as I find Woody the Woodchuck our problem will be solved. Don't go anywhere, I'll be right back." Willie yelled to Rachael as she hopped off, "It'll never work; how we are going to get that big tree down?" To which Rachael responded as she ran off into the distance toward Woody's home, "Stop being negative—every problem has a solution—you just have to be creative! In the meantime, I've gotta go find our friend Woody. See you soon." Within minutes, Rachael came back with Woody and a few of his woodchuck friends. It didn't take long for Woody and his friends to nibble their way through the tree trunk. With one last bite from Woody, the big tree tumbled down on to the other side of the creek. Everyone ran across to enjoy the delicious walnuts and berries all afternoon long until they were so full they couldn't eat another morsel. As Willie took his last bite, he looked up at Rachael and said, "I suppose you were right, every problem does have a solution." Willie looked at Rachael and said, "Now I need a solution to my next problem—what do I do to make my belly stop hurting; I ate too much!"

Kid M.E.A.L.S.

CREATIVITY

Story #2

Creative Play

[Age 3-4] Here's a Story to help your child think about creative ways to spend their time when they're stuck inside the house.

Willie the Worm and Sammy the Squirrel were playing outside one afternoon with their good friend Shane (substitute with your child's name) in his brand new sandbox. Unfortunately, a big rainstorm spoiled all their fun, and forced them to have to go indoors until it passed through. They ended up back at Sammy's house complaining that there was nothing to do. The storm mad everyone very sad, because they were looking forward to playing in Shane's new sandbox all week long.

Sammy didn't want the rain to ruin his afternoon so he created a game that would cheer everyone up until it was okay to go back outside. He went into his toy closet, where he kept all his stuffed animals, and piled all of them up in the middle of the room. He said to Willie, "I've got a great idea! Let's pretend that this pile of stuffed animals is the sandbox in Shane's backyard." On the count of three they all dove into the pile of stuffed animals and rolled around the floor laughing and playing while they made believe the pile of stuffed animals was a big sandbox. They had so much fun playing that they never even realized it stopped raining outside.

CREATIVITY

Sky Stories

[Age 4-6] On a cloudy day, invite your child to go outside and make up "sky stories." Lie back on a blanket, or perhaps a hammock, and create a **S**tory based on the images playing out in the clouds above. For instance, you may see a dragon image that can be included in your **S**tory. When you're done telling your **S**tory, have your child take over by creating their own, based on what they see in the cloud figures. Resist the temptation to help them too much. The more you allow them to rely on you, the less likely they will be cultivating their own creative abilities. Don't forget to have fun!

As your child becomes more creative using their imagination, they will become more confident and capable of seeing things from more than one perspective. Sky **S**tories will help your children learn how to see things from several points of view, because even though the two of you might be looking at the same set of clouds in the sky, many times you will end up interpreting what you both see, differently.

Chapter 7

"Really, I'm fine. It was just a fleeting sense of purpose—I'm sure it will pass."

PURPOSE

pur•pose, n.—an aim or goal; determination.

The only true happiness comes from squandering ourselves for a purpose.

—William Cowper

Children can feel lost in our complex world. But you can use your power as a parent to help them find their place within it by instilling them with a sense of purpose. As they seek to satisfy their appetite that comes from such wonderment, you will find yourself answering such questions as: What happens to people when they die? Where does God live? Or, perhaps, they'll want to know their reason (purpose) for being here at all? Be prepared to deal with these concerns when they surface and guide them in positive directions. Don't hesitate to explore them with your children so they feel comfortable thinking and talking about them. It's a puzzle they should be encouraged to solve.

Their ties to family, community, religious beliefs, and cultural heritage are qualities of life that will give them a sense of identity, direction, and purpose. These facets of their life will instill meaning and beliefs that will answer many of their questions that come from their uncertainty about the world.

A sense of purpose instills value in a person's life. It stems from an appreciation of where they came from, why they are here, who they are, and where they wish to go. "PURPOSE" Kid M.E.A.L.S. give parents the power to begin nourishing these areas of your child's heart and mind.

Kid M.E.A.L.S.

PURPOSE — **M**essage

[Age 5+]   QUESTION of the Day

When you grow up, which would you rather be?

☐ Doctor   ☐ Athlete   ☐ Builder   ☐ Pilot

☐ Teacher   ☐ Other _____

PURPOSE

Picture the Future

[Age 5+] This Exercise teaches your child to set up goals by taking advantage of the power of pictures. Clip out a picture of something that you'd like your child to strive for. For example, if they are learning how to swim at the local YMCA, paste up a picture of an Olympic swimmer accepting a medal. Or, check with their teacher to find out about their midyear and end of year academic goals. If, for instance, it's addition and subtraction, paste up a math problem and explain to them that, by the middle of the school year, they'll be able to figure out how to solve the math problem. Once they accomplish their mid-year goal, praise them for their achievement, and carry over a similar Exercise into the back half of the school year. If one of their academic goals is being able to read, post a sentence on the refrigerator that reads, "Congratulations, John Ryan; if you know what this says, then you can read!"

If for some reason they do not reach their desired goal, it's important that you make them feel good about the progress they did make. At this age, it's important to develop their love of learning.

Kid M.E.A.L.S.

PURPOSE

Religion

[Age 3+] Nourishing your child's spiritual appetite will strengthen their belief system, instill them with wholesome values, and provide meaning and purpose in their lives. Teaching your child about God's presence anchors their heart and mind to a higher source of power and goodness.

A healthy supply of spirituality includes *prayer* and *participation in religious services* on a consistent basis. Not only will it enhance their relationship with God, it's also an excellent way to bond your family together, build strong tradition, and provide a sense of community for them. Making God an **A**ctive part of you're your family's lifestyle is one of the most valuable contributions you'll make toward enriching the quality of your child's life.

PURPOSE

Kid Contributor

[Age 6+] Putting aside our own needs and focusing on others broadens our concept of who we are and makes us feel good, because we are making a contribution to a larger cause. Help your child understand the value of doing things for a purpose that goes beyond their own interests by turning them into a "Kid Contributor". It's a great **A**ctivity that will extend a child's sense of purpose beyond themselves comes in the form of contribution. Choose a charitable organization, such as the Sunshine Foundation, which caters to terminally ill children, and encourage your child to set aside a few dollars each time he or she receives a gift or allowance for the charity of their choice. Save up the funds throughout a specified period of time in a separate jar marked with the name of the charity. Then, send the donation to the organization along with a handwritten note from you and your child. Involvement in this type of **A**ctivities expands their world and demonstrates how they can have a positive impact on the lives of others.

For a greater value, take time to visit the organization with your child, so they see their donation at work. Or, if that's not possible you can learn about the organization online or at your local library. Being a "kid contributor" will give their actions a purpose, make them feel valuable because of their contribution, and at the same time instill them with an appreciation for all they do have.

Kid M.E.A.L.S.

PURPOSE — Activity #3

Step with a Purpose

[Age 5+] This Activity requires the following supplies: plastic storage containers, a bag of ready-mix cement, rubber gloves for protection, an outdoor hose, and thin plastic kitchen wrap. Each member of the family will create their own stepping stone to remind them about which can be used as outside steps or displayed in a garden.

Working outdoors, mix the cement in seperate plastic bins—one for each person in the family. Once the cement begins to harden, cover it with a thin layer of the plastic wrap. Then, press into the cement with your bare hands and feet to form imprints into your stepping stone. Now, insert small object(s) into the cement that represent future goals. For example, your child may want to be a baseball player some day, so include a small baseball in the mold. Or, they may want to be a dancer, so insert a doll's tiny dancing shoes. If you are thinking about writing a book, insert a pen into your mold.

You're only limited by your own goals. It may even give you a reason to set a new one. Whatever it is, make it a part of your "step with a purpose."

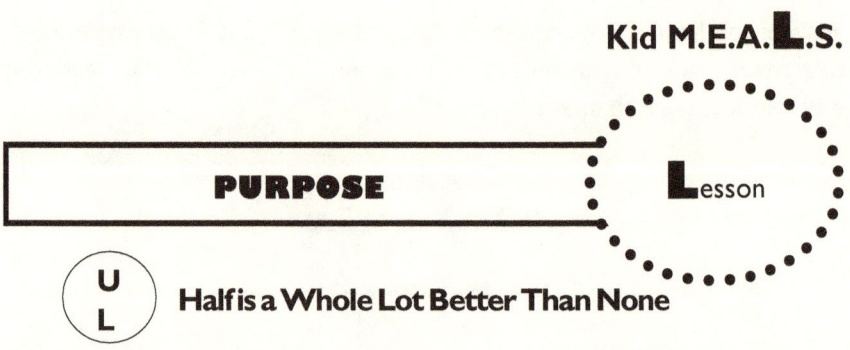

Half is a Whole Lot Better Than None

[Age 6+] Teach your child a Lesson that instills them with a purpose for helping others. Begin by having your child earn *two* dollars by completing an errand, such as cleaning their room. After they complete their chore thank them for doing their errands, and. let them know you recognize their effort for being responsible by handing them the two dollars.

Then, ask your child this simple question, "What is half of two dollars?" When they answer correctly (one dollar), follow up with this question, "Is one dollar better than none?" Agree with them when they say yes, and smile approvingly. Point out to your child that there are many children in the world who do not have enough money to even afford basic things, such as a warm meal. Further explain that, "one dollar will make your life a *little bit better*, but one dollar could make someone else's life a *whole lot better*. If you gave one to charity you'd still have one for yourself! You'd have half—which is a whole lot better than none, wouldn't you agree?"

It's here where you instill them with a purpose for helping others. Encourage them to donate one of the dollars that they earned for the sake of someone who needs it more than they do. Then, wait until you're out somewhere where they can place it into a charity container. As they do so let them know how proud you are of them by saying, "I know you probably wanted to keep that second dollar for yourself, but what you did was done for a very good purpose, and you should be proud of yourself. It is certain to make someone's life a whole lot better because you were so generous."

Later that week, once they've long forgotten about the dollar they donated, approach your child and ask them the same question you posed at service earlier in the week, "Is half better than none?" When they answer yes, hand them another dollar, and say, "This is for caring enough to donate some of your money to someone in the world who needed it a whole lot more than you and me."

Up-Link
<u>MOTTO of the Day</u>

Half is a Whole Lot Better Than None

Dream

[Age 4+] Your child's hopes and dreams for tomorrow will give them a purpose for living today. Dreaming is fun to do. Most adults are incapable of letting go of the hectic pace that dominates their day-to-day activity. They become so busy that they forget about the magic that comes from keeping their own hopes and dreams alive. Yet dreams can come true and you should encourage your child not to let go of their dreams. They instill us with a sense of purpose and supply us with one of life's greatest ingredients—the power to pursue the things we dare to dream are possible.

While driving together in the car or just hanging out in the backyard, take time to encourage your child to dream. Start with a **S**tory about how a dream of yours came true, not by accident, but through purpose of action. Then, ask your child to dream about what would make them happy. This will give emphasis to the idea that dreams are powerful—and give the future a purpose. Best of all, it will give them a reason to believe that dreams really do come true.

> *Somewhere over the rainbow . . .*
> *Skies are blue.*
>
> *And the dreams that you dare to dream . . .*
> *really do come true.*
>
> —E.Y. Harburg

♦ Last Course ♦

"... and God bless Mommy and Daddy. Amen. Over and out."

CONCLUSION

A hundred years from now it will not matter what my bank account was, the sort of house I lived in, or the kind of car I drove. But, the world may be different because I was important in the life of a child.

—*Anonymous*

I do not believe our children's future should be compromised in order to accommodate our over-worked society. If they are going to succeed, then today's generation of busy parents must be ambitious about finding ways to enhance the quality of time they spend developing their child's system of values. However, it won't be possible in today's time-deprived culture unless parents are motivated to find innovative, relevant, and effective ways to inspire them, in spite of their time-consumed schedules. *Parent Power* provides working and non-working parents with a formidable solution to this modern family dilemma. If parents do everything in their power to accomplish this goal, on behalf of their child's future, then they will have paved the way for them to live happy, rewarding, and fulfilled lives; thereby, enriching the value of their life, the life of others, and the world they live in.

Accepting this responsibility offers parents some of life's greatest rewards. Among them is the feeling that you get when you hear your child say, "I love you." Another is the sense of trust and companionship you feel when they come to you with their troubles, as well as their joys. However, the greatest feeling of all does not come from what you receive from them, it comes from what you give them, which is the most powerful gift in the world—knowing what it feels like to be loved.

INDEX

Academic, 67, 72, 76
    awareness, 69
    goals, 127
Accept, 32, 34, 40, 86, 97
    themselves, 34
Accomplishment, 30, 77, 119
Accountability, 101
Achievement, 127
Acknowledge, 99, 114
Adventure, 27, 45, 118
Adversity, 32
Affection, 49, 53, 61
Afraid, 44, 85, 93, 107
Angry, 63, 112
Appreciate, 37, 107, 110
Appreciation, 125, 129
Approval, 80
Aptitude, 76
Artistic, 110
Attention, 18, 21, 45, 47, 48, 57, 76, 99, 104, 114
Attitude, 21, 32, 72
Authentic, 32
Aware, 13, 21, 111

Bacal, Lauren, 107
Bad, 37, 81
    feelings, 64

Behavior, 13, 18, 83, 89, 91, 96
Belief, 21
    system, 128
Beliefs, 21, 125
Believe, 19, 30, 32, 42, 107, 133, 137
Blame, 58, 59, 86, 101
Bocchini, R. Richard, Ph.D., 14
Brave, 90, 93
Burden, 53, 72, 120

Caring, 132
Challenge, 13, 33, 69, 110, 120
Challenges, 27, 72
Change, 13, 18, 19, 41, 42, 72, 115
Character, 45, 95
Charades, 112
Characteristics, 13
Charity, 60, 129, 121
Cheat, 87
Child's
    future, 137
    interest, 21, 69
    perception, 77
    view of world, 117
Childhood, 20
Choices, 18, 91, 97
Choose, 33, 58, 69, 92, 97, 129
Clark, Jean Illsley, 20

Cognitive skills, 23, 67-80
Communicate, 23, 32, 36, 47, 49, 50, 58, 112
Communication, 35
Community, 117, 125, 127
Compare, 17, 40, 79, 87, 119
Compassion, 53, 60
Comprehend, 75
Confidence, 21, 27, 33, 35, 36, 37, 38, 54, 103, 107, 114, 119
Consequences, 93, 97
Consistent, 127
Control, 63, 97, 119
Cope, 62
Courage, 41, 42, 44, 86, 87, 90, 93, 107
Cowper, William, 125
Create, 36, 37, 110, 111, 115, 116, 119, 123
Creative, 13, 19, 23, 79, 96, 107, 113, 114, 116, 117, 118, 120, 122, 123
Creativity, 23, 107-123
Cultivate, 14, 27, 47, 83
Culture, 13, 137
Curiosity, 100

Decision, 91
   making skills, 97
   maker, 97, 98
Determined, 39, 42, 44, 120
Desire, 18, 21, 27, 32, 83
Difference, 40, 56, 57, 75, 101
Different, 92, 113, 123
   point-of-view, 107
Disappointment, 58, 62
Discouraged, 32

Discover, 34, 41, 42, 62, 107, 117
Dreams, 31, 133

Educate, 23
Educational, 19, 21, 67, 79, 117
Ego, 21, 34
Embarrassment, 64, 65, 87
Emotional, 13, 14, 18, 19, 47, 49, 91, 112
   breather, 55
   development, 13, 23, 20, 47—65, 61, 62
   foundation, 19
   level, 14
   pain, 58
   set backs, 62, 64
   stress, 53
Emotions, 21, 47, 53, 61, 64
Empathy, 60
Encouragement, 21, 32, 44
Enthusiasm, 18, 21, 69, 72, 114
Excuses, 101
Express
   affection, 49
   emotions, 61
   empathy, 60
   feelings, 61
   individuality, 107
   themselves, 35, 49, 107
Expressions, 112
Eye contact, 21, 33

Fail, 32, 58
Failure, 64
Family, 13, 17, 18, 35, 41, 87, 98, 115, 130, 137
Fear, 44, 54, 83, 93, 112

INDEX

Feel, 13, 30
    bad, 64, 65, 86
    valuable, 30, 129
Feelings, 21, 32, 36, 48, 64, 89
    of affection, 61
First aid, 103
Friendship, 9
Focus, 21, 56, 58, 62, 64, 76
Focusing, 28, 34
Forgive, 58
Foster
    intellectual confidence, 67
Full potential, 40, 75

Goals, 127
Guide, 69, 79, 125

Happiness, 125
Happy, 112
Honesty, 23, 83-93
Hope, 31, 123
Humor, 50

Identity, 125
Imagination, 108
Independent, 114
Individuality, 107
Intellectual, 18, 19, 20
    development, 20
    foundation, 19
    well-being, 67
Inspire, 21, 23, 97, 137
Integrity, 83
Interaction, 19, 20, 23

Joy, 18, 137

Kind, 34, 60

Listen, 21, 32, 37, 48, 91, 148
Listening, 21, 48, 105
    Skills, 21, 48
Lying, 86, 87, 88
Love, 9, 11, 19, 20, 22, 35, 45, 49, 52, 53, 56, 61, 80, 90, 127, 137

Message of the Day, 114
Mistakes, 32, 58, 86, 91
Motivated, 19, 22, 44, 137
Motivation, 83
Motto of the Day, 22, 23, 28, 44, 57, 92, 132
Name-calling, 63
Nature, 41, 43, 50, 62, 79
Negative, 34, 64, 121
Negativity, 32
New Yorker Artists
    Cheney, Tom, 125
    Dernavich, Drew, 106
    Kaplan, Bruce Eric, 82
    Lorenz, Lee, 66
    Opie, Everiett, 136
    Twohy, Mike, 16, 26, 46, 94
Nonverbal, 35

Opportunity, 18, 69, 71, 76, 95, 97, 98
Originality, 107
Over-inflated
    view, 22

Parenting, 14, 17, 18, 19, 20, 21
Patience, 9, 63

Peaceful, 55, 62
Perceived, 72
Perfect, 20
Personal
    development, 14, 17, 19, 21, 23, 47
    growth, 27
Perspective, 62, 117, 123
Playful, 73
Positive, 23, 28, 34, 60, 69, 72, 125
    attitude, 72
    attributes, 34
    behavioral development, 20
    force, 18
    impact, 129
    qualities, 36
    words, 49
Potential, 40, 75
Praise, 22, 56, 57, 127
Pressure, 17, 19
Pride, 11, 18, 30
Proactive, 56
Problem solving, 73, 120
Punishment, 87
Purpose, 23, 125-133
    of action, 133

Qualities, 9, 14, 18, 19, 23, 34, 36, 125
Quality, 9, 20, 21, 22, 27, 50, 76, 83, 107, 128, 137
    of time, 9, 14, 17, 18, 19, 20
    of attention, 18
Question of the Day, 22, 23, 28, 31, 68, 69, 73, 99, 126

Real, 95
Reinforce, 20, 23, 29, 119
Relax, 50, 51, 55, 62
Religion, 127
Resourceful, 100
Respect, 21, 89, 97
Responsible, 91, 93, 96, 98, 101, 131
Risk, 32

Sad, 64, 80, 85, 112, 122
Security, 103
Self
    confidence, 27, 95
    sufficient, 95, 96
    worth, 27
Self-esteem, 23, 27-45, 29, 35, 38
Self-reliance, 23, 95-105, 97, 100
Sense
    of accomplishment, 119
    of humor, 50
    of purpose, 125, 129, 133
    of responsibility, 98
Shame, 87, 120
Share, 64, 68, 89, 120
Sharing, 91
Shy, 34, 36, 60, 61, 115
Silently
    register, 21
    wondering, 31, 40
Sincere, 86
Solve problems, 72
Spirituality, 128
Strengthen, 21, 67, 128
Stress, 53
Stress-reducer, 53
Strive, 127
Success, 27, 32, 38
Successful, 18, 44, 47, 57, 77, 110
Supportive, 115
Suppressing

INDEX

feelings, 61
System, 128
    of values, 137

Teach, 11, 14, 21, 22, 23, 35, 38, 47, 53, 55, 58, 60, 61, 62, 67, 71, 74, 83, 89, 95, 103, 118, 127, 128, 131
Teacher, 126
Teasing, 63
Tradition, 128
True, 31, 37, 41, 43, 133
    happiness, 125
    self, 88
Trust, 32, 86, 90, 137
Truth, 85, 86, 87, 88, 89, 90, 93
Truthfulness, 83

Unhappy, 56
Uncertain, 41, 125
Unconditional love, 9
Unconditionally accept, 32
Understanding, 60, 72, 95, 103
Unique, 14, 23, 29, 30, 40
Uniqueness, 40
Up-link, 23, 31, 57, 73, 92, 99, 114, 132

Validate, 37, 48
Value, 13, 33, 45, 61, 75, 91, 95, 119, 125, 129, 137
    of believing, 45
    of care, 60
    of compassion, 60
    of forgiveness, 58
    of friendship, 9
    of honesty, 83, 93
    of humor, 50
    of integrity, 83
    of relaxation, 55
    system, 22
Valuable, 18, 20, 22, 27, 30, 89, 128, 129
    lesson, 9, 89
    messages, 22
Values, 13, 14, 23, 128
Verbal, 35
    Interaction, 76
    language, 112
    skills, 36
Verbalizing, 49, 56, 76

Wants, 32, 33, 34, 59
Weak, 41
Willie the Worm, 41, 44, 63, 64, 80, 91, 104, 120, 122
Winning, 80, 81
Wizard of Oz, 45
Word of the Day, 22, 23, 28, 48, 68, 84, 108
Worthy, 27
Wrong, 87, 90, 91

Ying & Yang, 91, 92

REFERENCES

Books

- *Beyond Success and Failure—Ways to Self-reliance and Maturity*, Willard and Marguerite Beecher (Pocket Books 1975)
- *Chicken Soup for the Kid's Soul*, Jack Canfield, Mark Victor Hansen, Patty Hansen, Irene Dunlap (Health Communications, Inc. 1998)
- *Coping Skills Intervention for Children*, Susan G. Forman (Jossey-Bass Publishers 1993)
- *Einstein Never Used Flash Cards*, Kathy Hirsh-Pasek, Ph.D. and Roberta Michnick Golinkoff, Ph.D. (Rodale 2003)
- *Father Need*, Kyle D. Pruett, M.D. (Broadway Books 2000)
- *Fathering—Strengthening Connection With Your Children No Matter Where You Are*, Will Glennon (Conari Press 1995)
- *How Good Parents Raise Great Kids*, Alan Davidson, Ph.D. & Robert Davison (Warner Books 1996)
- *How to Talk So Kids Will Listen & Listen So Kids Will Talk*, Adele Faber and Elaine Mazlish (Quill 1980)
- *Kindergarten Is Too Late!*, Masaru Ibuka (Fireside Books 1977)
- *Parenting for Dummies*, Sandra Hardin-Gookin and Dan Gookin (Hungry Minds 2002)
- *Playful Parenting*, Denise Chapman Weston, MSW and Mark S. Weston, MSW (Penguin Putnam Inc. 1993)
- *Preschooler Play & Learn—150 Games and Learning Activities for Children Ages Three to Six*, Penny Warner (Meadowbrook 2000)
- *Proactive Parenting—Guiding Your Child from Two to Six*, Faculty of Tufts University's Eliot-Pearson (Berkley Books 2003)
- *Raising an Emotionally Intelligent Child*, John Gottman, Ph.D. (Fireside Book 1997)

- *Raising Great Kids—Parenting with Grace and Truth*, Dr. Henry Cloud and Dr. John Townsend (Zondervan Publishing House 1999)
- *Raising Self-Reliant Children in a Self-Indulgent World*, H. Stephen Glenn, Ph.D. and Jane Nelsen, Ed.D. (Prima Lifestyles 2000)
- *Self-Matters*, Phillip C. McGraw, Ph.D. (Simon & Schuster Source)
- *Self-esteem Games—300 Fun Activities That Make Children Feel Good about Themselves*, Barbara Sher (John Wiley & Sons 1998)
- *The Childhood Roots of Adult Happiness*, Edward M. Hallowell, M.D. (Ballantine Books 2002)
- *The Field Guide to Parenting*, Shelley Butler and Deb Kratz (Chandler House Press 1999)
- *The Hurried Child—Growing Up Too Fast Too Soon*, David Elkind, Ph.D. (Persius Publishing 2001)
- *The Magic of Encouragement—Nurturing Your Child's Self-Esteem*, Stephanie Marston (Pocket Books 1990)
- *The Spirituality of Success—Getting Rich with INTEGRITY*, Vincent M. Roazzi (Brown Books 2002)
- *The Successful Child—What Parents Can Do to Help Kids Turn Out Well*, William Sears, M.D. and Martha Sears, R.N. (Little Brown & Company 2002)
- *The Don't Sweat Guide For Parents*, Richard Carlson, Ph.D. (Hyperion 2001)
- *The Essential 55*, Ron Clark (Hyperion 2003)
- *The Kidfun Acivity Book*, Sharla Feldscher and Susan Lieberman (Harper Perennial 1995)
- *The Quotable Dad*, Various Authors Edited by Nick & Tony Lyons (The Lyons Press 2002)
- *The 100 Simple Secrets of Happy People*, David Niven, Ph.D. (Harper 2000)
- *What Really Happens in School K-5*, Ann E. Laforge (Hyperion 1999)
- *Touchpoints 3 to 6*, T. Berry Brazelton, M.D. and Joshua D. Sparrow, M.D. (Merloyd Lawrence Book 2001)
- *What's Best for Kids—Practices for Teachers and Parents of Children Age 4-6*, Anthony Coletta, Ph.D. (Modern Learning Press 1991)
- *Working Parents' Survival Guide*, Sally Wendkos Olds (Prima Publishing 1989)

- *You Are Your Child's First Teacher—What Parents Can Do with and for Their Children from Birth to Age Six,* Rahima Baldwin Dancy (Celestial Arts Berkeley California, 2000)
- *10-Minute Life Lessons For Kids—52 fun and simple games and activities to teach your children and other important values,* Jamie Miller (Harper Perennial 1998)
- *10 Secrets for Success and Inner Peace,* Dr. Wayne Dyer (Hay House, Inc. 2001)
- *101 Secrets A Good Dad Knows,* Walter Browder & Sue Ellin Browder (Rutledge Hill Press 2000)
- *101 Ways to be a Special Dad,* Vicki Lansky (Contemporary Books 1993)
- *101 Ways to Build Self-Esteem and Teach Values,* Diana Loomans with Julia Loomans (HJ Kramer 1994, 2003)
- *101 Ways to Make Your Child Feel Special,* Vicki Lansky (Contemporary Books 1991)
- *104 Activities That Build: Self-Esteem,* Alanna Jones (Rec Room Publishing 1998)
- *365 fun-filled Learning Activities you can do with your child [3-7],* Mary Weaver (Adams Media Corporation 1999)
- *365 Ways to Build Your Child's Self-esteem,* Cheri Fuller (Pinon Press 1994)
- *365 ways to raise GREAT KIDS,* Sheila Ellison (Sourcebooks, Inc. 1998)

Web Sites

- Childlife
  http://www.childlife.com
- Child.com
  http://www.child.com
- Christian Parenting Today
  http://www.christianitytoday.com/parenting
- Early Childhood Today
  http://teacher.scholastic.com/products/ect/roots.htm
- Father's World
  http://www.fathersworld.com

- Focus on Your Child
  http://www.focusonyourchild.com/parentassess
- Growing Child
  http://www.growingchild.com
- Kids Health for Parents
  http://kidshealth.org/parent/emotions
- Kid Solutions
  http://www.kidsolutions.com
- Parenthood
  http://www.parenthood.com
- Parenting
  http://www.parenting.com/parenting
- Parenting With Confidence—PWC
  http://www.parenting.org.nz/aboutpwc/magazine.html
- Parents
  http://www.parents.com/index.jsp
- The Parents Journal
  http://www.parentsjournal.com/index.html

ABOUT THE AUTHOR

John graduated from Temple University in 1985 with a B.A. in broadcast communications. While he was studying, the International Radio & Television Society selected him as one of the nation's top twenty communications students. He entered the field of television broadcasting as an account executive with NBC affiliate, WMGM-TV, in Atlantic City, New Jersey. Four years later, he came back to Philadelphia to join the sales force with NBC affiliate, KYW-TV. While there, he returned to school part-time to pursue his M.B.A. at Temple University. In 1995, he transferred to the CBS Television Stations division in New York, NY. Two years later, he rejoined CBS 3 Television in sales management capacity, a position he has since held.

His wife of twelve years, Kathie, has also been employed in the communications industry since graduating from Penn State University with a B.A. in communications in 1987. She works full time in management for the nation's top television retail network—QVC, West Chester, Pennsylvania. They are the proud parents of seven-year-old John Ryan; four-year-old Shane Joseph; and eight-month-old, Maurina McKniff.

Born and raised in Philadelphia, Pennsylvania, John grew up with his identical twin brother, Philip, who now serves as a lieutenant colonel in the United States Air Force; and sister, Jo-Ann, who teaches for a private school in Philadelphia, Nazareth Academy. His parents just celebrated forty-five years of marriage.

www.ingramcontent.com/pod-product-compliance
Lightning Source LLC
Chambersburg PA
CBHW032124090426
42743CB00007B/455